THE WAY OF
KINGS

THE WAY OF
KINGS

ANCIENT WISDOM
FOR THE MODERN MAN

NATHAN CLARKSON

BakerBooks

a division of Baker Publishing Group
Grand Rapids, Michigan

Published by Baker Books
a division of Baker Publishing Group
PO Box 6287, Grand Rapids, MI 49516-6287
www.bakerbooks.com

Printed in the United States of America

Library of Congress Cataloging-in-Publication Data
Names: Clarkson, Nathan, author.
Title: The way of kings : ancient wisdom for the modern man / Nathan Clarkson.
Description: Grand Rapids, MI : Baker Books, a division of Baker Publishing Group, [2022]
Identifiers: LCCN 2021041029 | ISBN 9781540900241 | ISBN 9781540902108 (casebound) | ISBN 9781493433988 (ebook)
Subjects: LCSH: Young men—Conduct of life—Biblical teaching Miscellanea. | Young men—Religious life—Miscellanea.
Classification: LCC BV4541.3 .C53 2022 | DDC 248.8/32—dc23
LC record available at https://lccn.loc.gov/2021041029

This publication is intended to provide helpful and informative material on the subjects addressed. Readers should consult their personal health professionals before adopting any of the suggestions in this book or drawing inferences from it. The author and publisher expressly disclaim responsibility for any adverse effects arising from the use or application of the information contained in this book.

Published in association with The Bindery Agency, www.TheBinderyAgency.com.

Baker Publishing Group publications use paper produced from sustainable forestry practices and post-consumer waste whenever possible.

22 23 24 25 26 27 28   7 6 5 4 3 2 1

CONTENTS

INTRODUCTION

Created to Be Kings

We men were created to be kings. To rule the dominions we've been given with truth, justice, and love. To bring life to the land we live in and prosperity to the inhabitants who exist inside its walls. To fight evil when it crosses our borders and to diplomatically connect and support our neighbors and allies in the battles of this world.

We were made to be kings. But something has gone wrong.

Somewhere down the line we began believing we were made to be *the* king. To decide for ourselves what is right and wrong. To use our power and prowess for our own selfish gain. To hoard our wealth at the expense of others and to steal what is not ours. To not sacrifice for the ones we love but to hide and live in fear instead.

Because while we were given a throne, we wanted to sit on *the* throne. But only when the King of Kings rules over us, only when we allow the Lord of all to have authority over our rule, will the kingdoms he has entrusted to us succeed.

Through the following pages, I want to help you like others have helped me to become a more whole and integrated man. In addition to stories and thoughts, I will offer you practical tips, recipes, workouts, plans for kicking addictions, reading lists, style insights, dating advice, and road maps to following your dreams. I want to inspire your mind and heart so you can claim the life of the king God made you to be.

HOW TO READ THIS BOOK

In the past, when a king was nearing the end of his reign, he would often write letters to the incoming king. This was a way for him to pass on the things he had learned and discovered in his years to better serve and guide the new king as he took on the responsibility of ruling a domain.

We see this practiced in countless royal lines, and we see it in Scripture in places like Proverbs, where King Solomon wrote to his sons in hopes of imparting his knowledge, beginning many of his chapters with "My son . . ."

This book, too, was written as a collection of essays from an older king who has gained hard-earned wisdom and experience to a younger king who is beginning his journey.

Each chapter is broken down like this:

Essay. At the beginning of each chapter is an essay on a particular aspect of being a king, specifically a king under God and over the domain he has given us to rule in our lives. It offers a few thoughts and insights into things relevant to our walks as men of faith in a modern world.

King's Questions. After each essay are questions. These questions are designed to personalize the words and lessons in a way that will connect to us in our own lives.

Scripture Reading. Next is a Scripture passage to give us insight into what the Bible has to say on the subjects covered. We can ingest the Word of God in a way that speaks directly to the issues we might be facing.

King Tip. Lastly, at the end of each chapter is a life tip that has something to do with the subject explored in the essay. The tips offer fun activities, educational bits, recipes, how-tos, short stories, dating advice, questionnaires, book lists, and more.

This book can be read alone to receive solo encouragement or enjoyed by a group—a Bible study, a men's group, or two friends learning and growing together.

It can be read once daily to complete a forty-one-day guide (including the afterword) to beginning your journey to becoming king, or it may be read once weekly spread out over a year.

1 A Man after God's Own Heart

I've always had an affinity for King David. Being a pastor's kid, I knew all the prominent figures in Scripture, from Adam to Paul. And as amazing as each of these people were—as influential and important as their lives were—I felt like because of the struggles I faced and my mind/personality, I couldn't totally connect to their stories. But right in the middle of 1 Samuel, the book in Scripture where David's story is told, was where I often found myself drawn to as a young boy.

David, like me, was wild at heart. He had a proclivity for getting in trouble, running his mouth, and picking legendary fights with fabled foes. But in his heart, he desired to be good, to do what was right, to own his mistakes, and to be God's. He was a character I could connect with.

My mom always said I was out of the box. She said I was larger than life, just like David. And reading his story showed me how God used this flawed but dedicated man, not because David was perfect but because of the choice he made over and over again to turn his heart toward God. That gave me hope that God could do the same for me.

Despite David being quoted, admired, and regarded as a good man by many, he was deeply imperfect and broken. David stole another man's woman and even had her husband murdered.

So how is it that we still laud this man for his faith and character? Why is it that men who were more consistently moral are less known? How is it that God chose David's line to be the one through which he entered the world?

The Bible describes David as "a man after [God's] own heart" (1 Sam. 13:14). In the Psalms, we read David's raw, heartfelt, and unfiltered prayers to God. And while you'd think that in writing about himself he would put a positive spin on his life, ignoring the broken and bad and highlighting his more honorable accomplishments, instead he stands before God in his prayer naked, baring all, acknowledging his need for God's presence and the devastating mistakes that took him from it. In the Psalms, David calls to, petitions, and cries for God and his mercy, love, forgiveness, and friendship—not as a man who thinks he has earned it but as a child who calls out to his Father in need and want. A king with armies, women, might, and fame comes before God as a child: weak, in need, and begging.

I don't know for certain, but I wonder if this is why David is seen as a legendary man of God. Perhaps it wasn't his good or bad works that set him apart. Maybe all along the thing that God so loved was David's heart, which was turned toward his Creator in humility and desire—a desire above all things that existed on both his best and worst days.

I have tried to be good and will continue to do so, but I have also been bad and will continue to be bad. Living a life of purpose and having a story worth telling will never be about me being enough. It will be about choosing to be a man after God's own heart and kneeling before my Creator with all my good, bad, and ugly, realizing I need him—my Savior, Father, and friend.

Being the man I ought to be won't come from the things I do or don't do; instead, it will come out of a relationship with my Creator. A heart after God's own.

KING'S QUESTIONS

1. What does it mean to you to be a man after God's own heart?

2. Are you a man after God's own heart, or do you want to be one? If so, why?

3. What's keeping you from feeling like or becoming one?

Scripture Reading

Oh, the joys of those who do not
    follow the advice of the wicked,
    or stand around with sinners,
    or join in with mockers.
But they delight in the law of the LORD,
    meditating on it day and night.
They are like trees planted along the riverbank,
    bearing fruit each season.
Their leaves never wither,
    and they prosper in all they do.

But not the wicked!
    They are like worthless chaff, scattered by the wind.
They will be condemned at the time of judgment.
    Sinners will have no place among the godly.
For the LORD watches over the path of the godly,
    but the path of the wicked leads to destruction.

Psalm 1

KING TIP #1

Adventure Pack Checklist

Going on any adventure, quest, or camping trip takes careful planning, and perhaps the most important thing to contemplate is what to take with you. You can take only what you can carry, but one of those items might just be the thing that saves your life or makes the trip epic. Below is a list of things every adventurer should consider taking.

1. *Large backpack and bedroll/sleeping bag.* This goes without saying, but I said it anyway.
2. *One pair of sturdy pants.* Wearing a pair of sturdy pants will save room in your backpack, and they will last through whatever the adventure throws your way.
3. *One change of shirt/underwear/socks.* When one gets dirty, wear the clean one. Switch off if necessary.
4. *Reusable water bottle.* Water is the nectar of life, and a reusable bottle will ensure you will always have enough and can refill as needed.
5. *First aid kit.* You hope you won't need first aid, but it's better to have the kit and not need it than it is to need it but not have it.
6. *Ranger scarf.* The possibilities for this small item are endless. It can be used as a bind, sun guard, or tourniquet.
7. *Knife.* You will always have a need for a knife. You can choose between a folding or a fixed blade, both of which have their pros and cons, but bring one no matter what!
8. *Notepad.* Whether you are a poet, an artist, or just a jotter, a notepad will be necessary to write down important things like directions or just thoughts when the batteries on your digital devices die.

9. *Nonperishable food.* Whether it's canned beans, a bag of nuts, a pile of dried meat, or all three, food that doesn't go bad could be a lifesaver on your quest.

10. *Fire starter.* Having the ability to build a fire will make any cold night you spend in the wilderness much more bearable. Magnesium and flint are both good for starting fires. But be careful and follow local laws!

11. *Hand sanitizer.* Clean those hands!

12. *Disposable camera.* A disposable camera means no batteries to worry about and no selfies to scroll through but still all the ability to document your adventure.

Royal Blood

I remember looking through the pages of our family history as a kid. One of my relatives had put together a book bound in red leather that detailed my ancestry. The names and dates went back years and years. And close to the end of the book was a revelation that has changed how I see myself and the world. I found recorded evidence that I am a descendant of royalty. Though the lines have split and turned, I discovered that I was, in fact, related to kings. This might seem like an antiquated piece of useless trivia to some, but to my young heart, it meant something powerful: I had royalty in my blood and bones, and with that knowledge came the realization that my actions mattered. I was part of something bigger than myself.

In Romans 8:17, the apostle Paul writes, "And since we are his children, we are his heirs. In fact, together with Christ we are heirs of God's glory." This means that regardless of our earthly bloodlines, or lineage, if we are in communion with God, we are heirs and descendants of the most powerful, important, and long-lasting kingdom—the kingdom of heaven.

God has not just begrudgingly accepted us to live as lowly workers or slaves of his kingdom. Rather, because of his offer of adoption, because of his gift, we have been invited into a spiritual bloodline of royalty. When we allow God to rule over us, we are given the right to be part of the royal family and to rule with him as kings.

Realizing we are royalty isn't simply a fun little thing to discover in an ancestry test. Discovering we are royalty will change everything about us. It will put us in a context where our choices matter more than we've ever realized before. Embracing our royalty will transform how we see ourselves, taking our self-perception from one of self-loathing, insecurity, and low status to one of healthy self-love, confidence, and importance. It will help us see who we truly are, who we were meant to be, and what we were created to do.

We are royalty not because of something we've done but instead because of the lineage and inheritance that has been given to us.

No matter who you are—your financial or professional status, what you look like, where you're from, or what you can do—you have been offered a bloodline of royalty from the King of Kings himself. Will you take up your crown?

KING'S QUESTIONS

1. How does it feel to know you've been invited to a royal lineage?
2. Would accepting royalty change how you live? Why?
3. Do you truly believe we were made to be kings?

Scripture Reading

The LORD said to my Lord,
   "Sit in the place of honor at my right hand
until I humble your enemies,
   making them a footstool under your feet."

The Lord will extend your powerful kingdom from
   Jerusalem;
      you will rule over your enemies.
When you go to war,
      your people will serve you willingly.
You are arrayed in holy garments,
         and your strength will be renewed each day like the
            morning dew.

The Lord has taken an oath and will not break his vow:
      "You are a priest forever in the order of Melchizedek."

Psalm 110:1–4

KING TIP #2

Essential Manners Every King Should Know

There are a few manners that every man should know and practice,
whether he is at a fancy party or just out and about. Having these
manners will set you apart as a man of value and help others feel
valued at the same time. They will also help you build important
relationships and cause others to feel important.

1. *Shaking hands.* A handshake conveys a lot about a person.
   When shaking hands, make sure to reach out with confidence, grasp firmly (not enough to cause pain), and release
   after one short squeeze.
2. *Making eye contact.* Looking people in the eye can change
   your entire reputation. It conveys confidence and lets
   the person you are talking to know they are being heard.
   Make sure that when you are talking to someone, you look
   the person opposite you in the eye, breaking occasionally
   for thought or to look at another person.

3. *Saying please and thank you.* Saying please and thank you is something everyone should've learned as children but many still don't practice. Saying please when asking for something and thank you when something is given to you can make you infinitely classier, and both of these things give honor to others.

4. *Offering to help.* Offering to help is an essential way to show you are a man of class. It doesn't have to be with grand gestures: even offering to wash dishes, carry something heavy up the stairs, or get something off the top shelf will drastically affect people's perception of you and is a small way to show the goodness inside of you.

5. *Displaying proper table manners.* There is an endless number of arbitrary table manners you can learn, but the ones that ensure you are a man of class include putting your napkin in your lap, waiting for the host to eat before you start, using your utensils and not your hands, not making bodily noises at the table, and accepting seconds if offered.

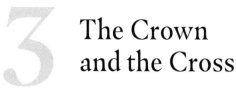

The Crown and the Cross

It's an amazing feeling to realize we're royalty—our name has power and we have been given influence over the world and circumstances around us. The saying "I feel like king of the world" is a common one that aptly describes the everyday feeling when life is under our control and going our way as a result of our decrees. But there's another part of accepting a crown that isn't as popular. There's a part of becoming a king that doesn't look like the triumphant, comfortable, leisurely life we often envision.

The cross.

The God of heaven came to earth. The Creator of everything in the universe stepped away from his throne in heaven and into our midst to save us, love us, and establish a new kingdom on earth: the kingdom of heaven. Jesus talked about this often in his thirty years here on earth. He talked about this new kingdom while performing miracles, teaching, healing, loving, and he also talked about it as he was lied about, tortured, betrayed, and on his way to be crucified. Jesus was and is King, but his reign came with a cross—one he took willingly.

Every crown comes with a cross; every reign comes with a responsibility.

Scripture tells us, "When someone has been given much, much will be required in return" (Luke 12:48), but what does that mean in the context of the kingdom God has asked us to help rule? What does that look like practically in the world? For Jesus it meant taking up his crown and receiving glory but also being killed by the ones he loved. Maybe for you it's taking on a new and more prominent position but also more stress and bigger responsibilities. Maybe it's the decision to get healthy that comes with the hardships of exercising and self-control. Maybe it's dealing with your mental illness but having to face the difficulty of opening up to a mentor or therapist. Maybe it's finding a wife but also accepting the difficulties of unconditionally loving and taking care of a family.

God has offered each of us a crown, but with it comes a cross. He does not force us to take either, but should we want to reign with him, should we want to take our place as royalty, it will also require sacrifice.

When Jesus tells us, "My yoke is easy to bear, and the burden I give you is light" (Matt. 11:30), his words can ring hollow. This life can often feel so, so heavy—almost too heavy for us to bear. But perhaps Jesus knew what we often forget: that yes, the yoke or cross is light not because it isn't heavy but because of his sacrifice.

Like a yoke on his back, Jesus carried the cross on which he would die. It was a weight as heavy as the world, but one he bore knowing it couldn't compare to the glory of the crown he would wear as he defeated death. It's in this story that we find the God who modeled for us both wearing his crown and bearing the cross.

KING'S QUESTIONS

1. Are you willing to accept both the crown and the cross?
2. As a result of following God, what have you found in your own life that is a crown?
3. As a result of following God, what have you found in your own life that is a cross?

Scripture Reading

The LORD is my shepherd;
  I have all that I need.
He lets me rest in green meadows;
  he leads me beside peaceful streams.
  He renews my strength.
He guides me along right paths,
  bringing honor to his name.
Even when I walk
  through the darkest valley,
I will not be afraid,
  for you are close beside me.
Your rod and your staff
  protect and comfort me.
You prepare a feast for me
  in the presence of my enemies.
You honor me by anointing my head with oil.
  My cup overflows with blessings.
Surely your goodness and unfailing love will pursue me
  all the days of my life,
and I will live in the house of the LORD
  forever.

Psalm 23

KING TIP #3

Mastering the Art of Conversation

The art of conversation, whether with important figures, friends, or colleagues, can set you apart, give you influence, and enable you to connect with the people around you in powerful and effective ways. Here are a few tips to becoming a master of the art of conversation.

1. *Be a good listener.* When you learn how to actively listen and really hear the people around you, you will be able to stay engaged in the conversation. The person you are talking to will also probably feel seen and valued.

2. *Ask a lot of questions.* Questions are the secret fuel to any great dialogue. Though most people think they should state things, asking questions will allow you to keep the conversation going and people engaged. Who doesn't like being asked questions about themselves?

3. *Have an opinion.* Sharing your point of view can be scary. You may worry you might not come across well or sound smart/good enough. But it's only when you find the confidence to share how you see the world and the other person that others feel they know you! The secret is sharing humbly and kindly.

4. *Think about your body language.* Though silent, body language speaks volumes. No one wants to talk with someone who looks bored, disinterested, or closed off. Making eye contact, nodding your head, uncrossing your arms, leaning in, and even offering the occasional "hmm" will affect those around you in a powerful way.

There Be Dragons

Dragons have made an appearance in almost every nation, culture, and mythos. We read about them in Scripture, where they are described as great creatures that breathe fire from their mouths and have scales on their skin. And we see them even today in movies, television shows, and books. Dragons have meant and still do mean something to us. Whether we realize it, something in the mythos of dragons connects to us and our stories even though none of us have actually seen one.

I remember as a young boy excitedly going over the pages of a picture book that detailed the story of Saint George and the Dragon. Saint George, in shining armor, takes up his sword at the request of a beautiful maiden to slay the dragon that has laid waste to her city. I can remember my intrigue as my eyes pored over every detail of the illustrations of Saint George confronting the towering beast. He is so small compared to the dragon, but nevertheless, he raises his weapon to take on the evil in front of him. He fights with courage, swinging his sword, but after a short while into the battle, the dragon's claws tear through his armor, and for a moment, all seems lost. But after retreating and being bandaged by the fair maiden, Saint George heads back to battle to finish the war once and for all. Wounded, hurt, tired, and weary, he lets out one last cry and charges and defeats his dragon.

In my young mind, I didn't know why this story captured my heart so deeply. Now I have more of an idea. I think perhaps I knew that soon, down the line, I would be facing my own dragons, and I needed to see that while the battle would be difficult, I, like Saint George, could win the fight.

We each will be given dragons to wrestle in our lives. Our dragons most likely won't look like Saint George's dragon. They most likely won't breathe fire or have razor-sharp talons. But they will be real.

No, our dragons won't look like dragons from the storybooks and movies. Our dragons will come to us in more insidious disguises, crashing into our world in the form of depression, oppression, loss, family dysfunction, abuse, lies, addictions, heartbreak, mental illness, regret, shame, and isolation. And while they don't look like the monsters from books, know that they will try to destroy us and take all the treasures life offers us.

But like the great stories of old, even though our dragons are big and scary and powerful, we as kings battling beside the one true King can overcome them. Yes, we might get cut, we might get wounded by the dragon's talons, but our God will bandage us up, send us back out, and wage war alongside us until the dragon has been slayed. We each are fighting and will continue to struggle against dragons in our lives. But know this: we aren't engaging the enemy alone. And with God by our side, we will overcome.

KING'S QUESTIONS

1. What is the greatest battle in your life right now? What makes it so difficult?
2. What ways do you feel you are winning, and what ways do you feel you are losing?
3. How does it feel to know God is rooting for and fighting with you?

Scripture Reading

O LORD, oppose those who oppose me.
  Fight those who fight against me.
Put on your armor, and take up your shield.
  Prepare for battle, and come to my aid.
Lift up your spear and javelin
  against those who pursue me.
Let me hear you say,
  "I will give you victory!"
Bring shame and disgrace on those trying to kill me;
  turn them back and humiliate those who want to harm
    me.
Blow them away like chaff in the wind—
  a wind sent by the angel of the LORD.
Make their path dark and slippery,
  with the angel of the LORD pursuing them.
I did them no wrong, but they laid a trap for me.
  I did them no wrong, but they dug a pit to catch me.
So let sudden ruin come upon them!
  Let them be caught in the trap they set for me!
  Let them be destroyed in the pit they dug for me.

Then I will rejoice in the LORD.
  I will be glad because he rescues me.
With every bone in my body I will praise him:
  "LORD, who can compare with you?
Who else rescues the helpless from the strong?
  Who else protects the helpless and poor from those
    who rob them?"

Psalm 35:1–10

KING TIP #4

How to Dress Wounds

Hopefully you'll never have a serious wound. But if you or someone you know does get hurt and you don't have immediate access to a hospital, here are the ways to dress different kinds of wounds. This is essential information for the adventurer.

A burn. A burn wound (either from a dragon or a campfire) can be a painful experience. To take care of such a wound, follow these steps:

1. Rinse the area under cool water.
2. If you have it, use an antibiotic ointment or aloe vera on the burn.
3. Place a clean nonstick bandage on the affected area.

A cut. Whether outdoors or inside, you may find yourself with a nasty cut that must be addressed immediately to mitigate pain and keep you from losing blood. Should you find yourself with a deep cut, follow these steps:

1. Stop the bleeding by applying firm pressure to the cut with a clean bandage or T-shirt.
2. If needed, apply a tourniquet, like a belt, above the wound to stop the bleeding.
3. Clean the wound using fresh water, ridding the area of *all* dirt and debris.
4. Sanitize the area with rubbing alcohol if you have it; then apply antibiotic ointment.
5. Apply a bandage, a gauze, or a clean T-shirt to the wound and fasten in place with tape, a belt, or your hand. Secure tightly but loosely enough to keep some circulation.

6. Elevate the wound.

7. Get professional medical attention ASAP.

A bruise. If you experience a hard hit either from a foe or a fall, you might develop a nasty bruise. Follow these steps to best address this type of wound:

1. Apply a cold compress to the injury. Do not put ice directly on it; instead, wrap the ice in a clean cloth or use a bag of frozen vegetables.
2. Apply for up to ten minutes at a time until the swelling reduces.

Damsels in Distress

Much ancient poetry and tale, be it written by king or commoner, has been about love. Through brilliant prose, flowing verse, and detailed descriptions that use image-inducing adjectives, we see how powerful the element of romance is—and both the positive and counterproductive effects it can have on the world and those who live in it. In Scripture, the sweeping romance of the book we call Song of Songs follows Proverbs, a book filled with warnings about youthful desires and foolish endeavors.

An example of destructive romantic desire can be found in the story of King David, who was almost taken down by his misuse of power and his corrupted desires by giving in to his lust for a beautiful woman he saw bathing on a roof. Then in Esther we see an entire nation saved through what some might call a romance of sorts. Love is a wild and wonderful thing. Like fire it can bring light, warmth, and life. However, unbridled love or lust devoid of love can destroy cities and take down even the mightiest of men.

We were designed for love. Sewn into our hearts and minds is a desire for passion, intimacy, and romance; to love and be loved; to seek out and be sought out; to share mind, body, and soul with another. Though many have looked for this love in these modern times, it seems harder and harder to find—at least the type that brings with it strength and not destruction. And some of us never find it at all.

Imitations of romance promise to fulfill our deep heart desires, whether they occur on our computer screens or in hollow one-night encounters that leave us more desperate than ever. We live in a world that has removed the grandness and passion from love and intimacy altogether, giving us nothing more than a knockoff drug to temporarily satisfy for a night what was meant to be a deep and lifelong desire found inside an unconditional, loving relationship protected by commitment.

So as kings, how do we find this thing we've read about in great books and seen in classic films? How do we begin the search for the true answer to this desire that God has placed in our hearts?

First, we don't accept the low and cheap view of love and intimacy the world often gives us. Maybe for some of us that means deleting the apps or shutting off the computer and instead learning to begin the search for a deeper, more beautiful and fulfilling romance, even when it will take more effort and be harder to find; after all, every great treasure is.

Then we must act in an honorable and upstanding way. We start by treating every woman as a whole and valuable person, not an object to use for a night or for visual pleasure. We learn to pursue the heart of a woman, and we follow God's wisdom for how to nurture relationships.

To be a king of worth, we must learn the ancient way of love, intimacy, and romance.

KING'S QUESTIONS

1. Do you think that sex and intimacy are sacred things? Why or why not?

2. Have you treated women in a way that doesn't honor them the way God asks us to? How and why?

3. What are some practical ways you can live out a higher view of love than the ways the world does?

❧

Scripture Reading

So now, my sons, listen to me.
    Never stray from what I am about to say:
Stay away from her!
    Don't go near the door of her house!
If you do, you will lose your honor
    and will lose to merciless people all you have achieved.
Strangers will consume your wealth,
    and someone else will enjoy the fruit of your labor.
In the end you will groan in anguish
    when disease consumes your body.
You will say, "How I hated discipline!
    If only I had not ignored all the warnings!
Oh, why didn't I listen to my teachers?
    Why didn't I pay attention to my instructors?
I have come to the brink of utter ruin,
    and now I must face public disgrace."

Drink water from your own well—
    share your love only with your wife.

Proverbs 5:7–15

KING TIP #5

Asking a Woman Out

When embarking on the nerve-wracking and exciting adventure of asking a woman out, you may have some doubt and fear and wonder how to go about it in the right way. Below is a simple guide to the first steps of getting to know a woman in a romantic context that will give you the best chance at finding a soul mate, while engaging her mind and heart and protecting both in the process.

Decide who to spend time with. Before you invite a woman on a date, ask yourself if she is someone who shares your values, interests, and beliefs. Determining this ahead of time will make sure no one's time is wasted. Search out someone to whom you are not only physically but also mentally and spiritually attracted. Before asking her out, make sure you have connected on more than just a surface level. Having had a couple meaningful conversations can make all the difference before you dive in.

Extend the invitation. Asking a woman out is one of the scariest things a young man can face. The key is to approach it with confidence. When the time has come, be direct. Don't allude or expect her to pick up hints. State your intentions, something like, "I'd like to take you on a date sometime. What do you think?" This way there is no confusion, and it shows confidence. If she says no, honor her decision, keep your head up, and continue to be friendly and polite. You might even make a great friend. Otherwise it will be obvious you showed care for her only when you thought you might get something romantically out of the deal. If she says yes, move on to the next step.

Have a plan. If you get a yes, don't drop the ball here! Have some suggestions ready for where you plan on going. Having an idea of what you want to do (perhaps suggest a specific activity) will take the pressure off both of you and give you and her more peace about what's going to happen. In addition, a man who has thought ahead is infinitely more appealing than one who hasn't, since it says a lot about the overall picture of his life. After all, if he can't even prepare for a date, how could we expect him to plan for a life? Since you extended the invitation, you should initiate some ideas about activities you could do together. See what sounds best to her. Below are some tweakable phrases you could use.

> "There's a great _____ I've been wanting to try. Does that interest you? When would you be free to hang out there?"

> "I've been wanting to see _____. I heard you express interest as well. What day works for you?"

> "I'd love to hear/talk more about_____. What do you think? When would you be free to get some dinner and continue our conversation?"

6 The Royal Council

Often when we hear the stories of kings, presidents, and rulers throughout history, in our limited perspective they appear to have accomplished great feats on their own. But if we take a closer look at any influential figure in history, we almost always find that they had help.

Curia regis is the Latin term for "royal council." It is a term that originated about a thousand years ago and was used to describe a special position of councillors and advisors to the kings of Normandy and England. The royal council held positions of authority in which they provided insight, wisdom, and perspective to whomever sat on the throne.

History is filled with stories of both good and bad leaders, but one of the common threads I have seen in the ones we consider great is that they surrounded themselves with wise councillors and advisors—their own *curia regis*.

A good king knows the weight of his decisions on the world and is well acquainted with his humanity. He knows we each have limited insight and that to rule well, we must humble ourselves to hear the perspective of others.

In Scripture, we see King David had his own *curia regis* throughout his reign in the form of both political advisors and prophets. For example, he valued people like Nathan (my namesake), who would call David back to God's truth when he strayed. David, in his humility, was willing to listen to others around him.

If we seek to be good leaders of our kingdoms, we cannot do it alone. It takes humility as well as strength to admit this. To rule our lives well, we must seek out and turn our hearts toward insight from wise individuals around us. We must find our own *curia regis*.

This will look different in our lives than it did for the kings of old, but the principle still stands. For us to rule well, we must allow the voices and insight of others into our lives. These voices might come from our fathers and mothers, or perhaps from a church or work mentor we meet with once a month. Or maybe the voice is a therapist who can offer a listening ear and a wise word in our stressful lives.

Whoever it is, whatever form it takes, we must find our own *curia regis*.

KING'S QUESTIONS

1. Do you have wise friends around you? If so, what makes them wise?
2. What are some practical reasons you think it helps to have a strong council around you?
3. How do you live differently when you have wise people around you?

Scripture Reading

Walk with the wise and become wise;
associate with fools and get in trouble.

Proverbs 13:20

KING TIP #6

How to Find a Mentor

Finding a mentor might be one of the most important aspects to your success. Finding someone who will share the wisdom, knowledge, and insight from their experiences is valuable. But how do you find such a person? Here is a list of ways to go about finding a mentor/counselor in your life.

1. Identify what you need in a counselor. In what ways would you like to grow? What things do you want to know more about that will help you in your calling?

2. Look for people who are further along in their career or life circumstances who will have insight to give you. If you are an entrepreneur, find someone who is accomplished in the business world. If you are pursuing the arts, look for an artist further along the path.

3. Find the type of mentor you are looking for by putting yourself in groups and communities that are centered around the things God has put on your heart.

4. Take care to let only wise people who have a history of healthy relationships, endeavors, and choices speak into your life. Look for people whom others speak highly of and who display honesty, kindness, wisdom, and success.

5. Be specific about what you are looking for. State up front that you are looking for someone who can provide insight into the particular area of your life where you want to grow, and politely ask if they would have some time to meet regularly.

6. Be humble when meeting. Let go of your pride so your mentor/counselor can help you. They will have experience and insight you don't have and could learn from.

Allow them to speak honestly to you, and learn how to listen without fighting back in the moment, even when you might not agree.

7. Take their advice. Find ways to practically implement their advice in your life and practices. You might just see the growth and development you have been looking for.

8. Thank them for their time. It's a sacrifice of time and energy to mentor someone. Let them know you appreciate them building into you.

9. If you're having a hard time finding a mentor, keep searching. This is important. And if you have the means, look into getting professional counseling or coaching. The process can yield unbelievably positive results.

7 The Round Table

Perhaps most of us have heard of King Arthur and the Knights of the Round Table. Whether historical fact or popular myth, the round table was a place King Arthur created and where he invited his friends and fellow kings to sit and commune. According to legend, the table was made round so there was no head—no one greater, no one lesser. Just kings communing for the good of their individual realms.

In the early part of the story of King David in Scripture, David is befriended by a young man named Jonathan. The writer describes them as closer than brothers, and as a result of their friendship, Jonathan actually ends up saving David from Jonathan's own father, who was trying to kill David.

Friendship was as important in the ancient stories of kings as it is today for us. The strength and necessity of connection and friendship bonds seems almost obvious. So many studies point to how important community is for the health of our minds and bodies, and regularly we see the negative effects on people and the world when there is a lack of connectedness. There's a true destructive nature to isolation, loneliness, and separation from others that can lead to depression, self-harm, violence, and sometimes suicide.

To live into our potential as kings, we must open ourselves up and invite friendship. We must create and join round tables where we can find them. It's hard in a world that can feel isolating, but it's needed for us to rule and live well.

It's not an easy thing to find one friend, much less a group of fellow kings. But we must try, because it has the power to strengthen our hearts, bring joy to our lives, and support our walk. Practically, that might look like joining a book club on campus or small group at church. It could be volunteering for a cause you feel strongly about where you'll meet other kindred spirits who care about the things you do. Or maybe it's starting a podcast about something you love that will draw other people with the same passions.

In every season of my life, though it was sometimes hard, I have sought out friends to walk this path with. Sometimes it's just seeing a movie once a week or discussing life over a cheap meal. And sometimes it's working with someone on a project—dreaming, thinking, and moving toward great things together. Every time I seek out, engage with, and connect to a friend, I am strengthened in the life God has called me to live.

We kings were made for comradery and connection, and when we find them, we will rule all the better knowing that we walk with other kings. So whatever your round table looks like, make the most of it.

KING'S QUESTIONS

1. Do you want to have a community of friendships around you? Why or why not?
2. What are some ways you can seek deeper friendships?
3. How do you think having those relationships will help you?

Scripture Reading

As iron sharpens iron,
so a friend sharpens a friend.

Proverbs 27:17

KING TIP #7

Hosting a King Cave Get-Together

Some of the best memories are made and the deepest souls shaped by gathering with like-minded men and forging friendships through deep conversations, full laughs, and loving encouragement. Here are a few ideas for hosting your own meeting of kings that will foster fun and ensure a memorable time will be had by all.

1. *Game night.* Game nights always please a crowd and get some healthy competition going! Get together some of your favorite snacks (or grill, if you dare) and drinks (craft root beer always goes over well), set out a table and chairs, and invite the guys over to play some games. Whether it's cards, Risk, Catan, or video games, play something that's engaging and leaves room for good conversation and connection. Get ready for the night to last for hours.

2. *Movie night.* Watching an epic or controversial movie is always a great bonding experience. Choose one that will either inspire the group or create good conversation. Load up on popcorn, turn off the lights, and after the movie is done, come up with some good questions to get you all talking.

3. *Dinner party.* Kings are known for their feasting, so what better way to spend an evening than with close friends and great food? Set up a table with a place for each guy and serve the food in courses (this makes the event more special and paces the evening). Make something filling, and have some questions to ask everyone between courses.

4. *Bonfire.* If you live in or near a place that allows a bonfire, this can be one of the most memorable and warrior-like activities to share with friends. There's nothing like sitting around a fire beneath the stars in the great outdoors (or even a backyard) sharing stories, thoughts, prayers, and laughs. Just have some metal hangers, a lot of hot dogs, and some s'mores ingredients prepared, and you're ready.

5. *Book club.* A book club is a great way to organize an ongoing community of guys. Gathering regularly to discuss thought-provoking or inspiring books can lead to deep conversations, exciting thoughts, and closer friendships. Check out the book lists in this book for ideas (see pp. 48–49 and 144).

8 Warrior Training

In almost every movie and book about heroes, whether it's *Batman*, *Star Wars*, *Hercules*, or *Mulan*, the hero of the story—before they even become the hero—goes through a time of training. Often there's grand music and slow-motion shots of them failing and succeeding as they hone their skills, powers, and particular strengths. Often this comes in the form of a cheesy montage, but this idea of preparation is an integral part of the hero's path, for this is the time when the hero is training for the challenges they will face.

Long ago, special training was part of being in a royal family. From a young age, princes and princesses, future heirs to the throne, were prepared for their positions in a myriad of ways. They were taught diplomacy, history, fighting skills, and other information that would make them capable of fulfilling their life's calling as royals.

Just like with the royals, part of our growth as kings means leaning into our training and development. Perhaps this will look less like the movies and books we've seen and read, but the discipline of training is nonetheless vital to our living into the story *we* are called to embrace.

God has called each of us to rule and live in a unique narrative, even in modern times. It will look different for every king, so we must tailor our training to our own unique story. For me, that was acting. I had big dreams of being a great actor on stages and screens across the world. But before I was ready to be a leading man, I had to take classes, read books, and practice in small ways what God had waiting for me so when the day came to live in and rule my domain, I was prepared.

Before famously defeating Goliath in battle and going on to be a great king, David spent his time as a shepherd in the fields. He learned the Scriptures, practiced protecting and leading sheep, and honed his fighting skills on wild animals. He ended up killing a bear and a lion! Look it up in 1 Samuel.

We must do the same. While we might want to just be "there" already, right now is the time to start preparing and training so that when we do arrive at the story we've been called to tell and the kingdom we've been given to rule, we will be prepared to do it well.

Don't wait for a later time to begin laying the groundwork. Start now, on this day. Pick up that book, go for that run, take that class. You have a story to tell. Now is the time to train so you will tell it well when you are ready.

KING'S QUESTIONS

1. What skill or calling do you love that you want to dedicate more time to?
2. Do you think training is important? Why or why not?
3. How can you find more time to invest in your passions?

Scripture Reading

Work brings profit,
  but mere talk leads to poverty!

Wealth is a crown for the wise;
  the effort of fools yields only foolishness.

Proverbs 14:23–24

KING TIP #8

Simple but Effective Workout Routine

Very few of us have the time or resources to get as buff as the superheroes we see in the movies. But there are realistic ways we can grow physically stronger with just a few hours of exercise a week. Below is a simple and quick workout routine for use at your local gym that will help you get stronger by focusing on the most important muscles.

Chest: The bench press is a classic move used by both beginners and weight lifters around the world. It will work out your entire chest/pectoral area while also working some muscles in your arms.

Arms: Curls are about the most popular workout for arms, focusing on those biceps everyone wants! They're simple but effective. And when done slowly and with good form, curls will shape your arms in no time.

Abs: An inclined sit-up is super tough at first, but as you go along you can start adding weight on your chest, and with a little dedication you will develop a strong core. This move works all the major ab and stomach muscles.

Legs: A squat is not fun, but it's easy and will yield huge results, especially as you grow stronger and add weight. You might look silly squatting up and down, but adding this exercise to your routine will ensure you a strong set of legs and core muscles.

Just doing these four exercises three times a week will be a great basic way to start building important muscle groups that will make you look and feel stronger. Start with a circuit of three sets of ten repetitions and add weight as you gain strength. And remember to keep good form!

9 The Quest

Every great protagonist, hero, king, and character from history, literature, movies, and comics had a mission to complete, a destiny to fulfill, a quest to accomplish.

In The Lord of the Rings trilogy, the secret king Aragorn and eight others venture to destroy an evil ring. In The Chronicles of Narnia series, the Pevensies discover and save a magical land called Narnia by reclaiming their throne after being called by Aslan. In Star Wars, Luke Skywalker discovers his status of Jedi and fights the dark side throughout the galaxy.

In history, read the tales of people like Joshua, God's chosen who led a nation through the desert and brought down the walls of Jericho; or Eric Liddell, the Scottish runner who won gold at the 1924 Olympics while honoring his faith; or Audie Murphy, a highly decorated American soldier who bravely fought an evil regime in World War II. Each had a calling on their lives that, when they followed it, led them to claim the status of legend.

As we claim and own the royal lineage we've been given, with it comes a calling. Our status as kings will come with a quest. God has written for each of us a story—a story that we have been called into with him to accomplish his work in the narrative he is and has been weaving for all time.

Taking hold of this idea will give us a new outlook on life. Knowing that we have been created for a story will encourage each of us to see our life as an important part of this world and will give our days purpose and our hearts hope.

We have a tale to tell, a destiny to fulfill. The quest we are given will be unique to us, our skills, and our passions; it will be specific to whom God has created us to be for the purpose he has given us. In the last chapter, we talked about training, but we don't train for the sake of training. We train so we will be equipped and ready to live out the story God has for us to tell.

For entrepreneurs this will be an opportunity to start movements and organizations that help the world and to run them with integrity and virtue.

For scientists, theologians, and thinkers this will be a quest to discover, learn, and share truth with the world in a way that brings glory to our Creator.

For teachers this will be a journey to ignite young minds to the love of learning and the joy that comes from understanding and education.

And for artists this will be a calling to create to the best of their ability the music, literature, film, and art that bring light and beauty into a dark and broken world.

Part of taking your throne is learning to get up off it and go. To venture confidently into the quest God has waiting for you. It will look different for each of us. But it will bring purpose and direction to the reign and stories we've been given.

KING'S QUESTIONS

1. Do you believe you were made for a great story? Why or why not?

2. What will it take for you to start living that out?

3. What epic stories inspire you?

Scripture Reading

The LORD directs the steps of the godly.
    He delights in every detail of their lives.
Though they stumble, they will never fall,
    for the LORD holds them by the hand.

Once I was young, and now I am old.
    Yet I have never seen the godly abandoned
    or their children begging for bread.
The godly always give generous loans to others,
    and their children are a blessing.

Turn from evil and do good,
    and you will live in the land forever.
For the LORD loves justice,
    and he will never abandon the godly.

He will keep them safe forever,
    but the children of the wicked will die.
The godly will possess the land
    and will live there forever.

Psalm 37:23–29

KING TIP #9

Fiction Book List

Sometimes to truly grasp the idea that you are made to live out a great story, you must read and fill your heart and mind with great stories. Below you'll find ten great stories to inspire you to live out yours.

1. The Lord of the Rings trilogy by J. R. R. Tolkien
2. The Chronicles of Narnia series by C. S. Lewis
3. *This Present Darkness* by Frank Peretti
4. Redwall series by Brian Jacques
5. The Green Ember series by S. D. Smith
6. The Wingfeather Saga by Andrew Peterson
7. *The Pilgrim's Progress* by John Bunyan
8. *Eragon* by Christopher Paolini
9. *Wrinkle in Time* by Madeleine L'Engle
10. Superman comics by Jerry Siegel and Joe Shuster

All ages and personalities can enjoy these tales. They will ignite your imagination and perhaps inspire you to live a great story in your life!

10 The King's Confession

I can only imagine the fear, shame, trepidation, and sadness that coursed through King David's veins as Nathan the prophet—his advisor, friend, and guide—confronted him about his secret and terrible murder and adultery. Scripture tells us David admitted to his sin, saying, "I have sinned against the LORD." Nathan told David, "Yes, but the LORD has forgiven you, and you won't die for this sin" (2 Sam. 12:13).

In the book of Psalms, we find David's numerous confessions and admissions of his failings. It's clear that while he was imperfect, David, over and over again, was willing to acknowledge and repent from his destructive choices. In his words are deep pain and true realizations of the ramifications of his actions on himself, others, and his relationship with God. Perhaps this is why he is honored with the title "man after God's own heart."

We each will fail miserably. We will make destructive choices that hurt ourselves and others and cause rifts in our relationship with our Creator. And as prideful kings and men, many times we want to hide, minimize, or escape the reality of our actions. But no matter how far we wander, our sin will find us out. And the longer we run, the more damage it will do.

God knows this, because he knows us. So instead of leaving us to our own devices, he offers each of us a gift. We follow a King who doesn't leave us in our mess but through his sacrifice for us offers forgiveness, redemption, and a way to be restored to the throne he has created for us. But this offer, while free, must be accepted, and it can be accepted only through our confession that we need his help in the first place.

To be good kings of our domains, we must realize the reality of our brokenness, offer confession for our human failings, and accept the loving forgiveness of our master. There is no other way to find healing and restoration. It's a humbling path for a king, but it's the only one that brings wholeness.

So often confession is seen as something weak that only messed-up or needy people do. But perhaps until we realize that we all have weak, messed-up parts and that we are all in need of a Savior, we won't find the freedom in our lives that we so long for.

Confession is integral to ruling well. When we find safe people and mentors to whom we can confess our sins and who, as God's hands, help us work through them, we can begin to be the kings we were made to be instead of the small, frightened rulers who will give up their domains to not be found out. Confession brings freedom and life.

So remember this: we have *all* fallen short of perfection. Paul says in Romans 3:23, "For everyone has sinned; we all fall short of God's glorious standard." And we will again. We're human and broken. But because of God's grace, we have a way forward, one available only through admitting our need for help. No matter what we've done or where we've been, we can be forgiven, be restored, and find freedom.

KING'S QUESTIONS

1. Do you think confession is good and/or necessary?
2. Is confession easy or hard for you? Why?
3. What do you feel you need to confess to God today?

Scripture Reading

From the depths of despair, O Lord,
    I call for your help.
Hear my cry, O Lord.
    Pay attention to my prayer.

Lord, if you kept a record of our sins,
    who, O Lord, could ever survive?
But you offer forgiveness,
    that we might learn to fear you.

I am counting on the Lord;
    yes, I am counting on him.
    I have put my hope in his word.
I long for the Lord
    more than sentries long for the dawn,
    yes, more than sentries long for the dawn.

O Israel, hope in the Lord;
    for with the Lord there is unfailing love.
    His redemption overflows.
He himself will redeem Israel
    from every kind of sin.

Psalm 130

KING TIP #10

Apologizing like a Man

When you have messed up and hurt someone, screwed something up, or just made an unintentional mistake, here are a few ways to reach out and say you're sorry with the best possible outcome in mind:

1. *Acknowledge.* The first step to saying you're sorry is actually acknowledging that you have done something that requires an apology. Sometimes even before you own this in front of others, you have to admit it to yourself. You must see that you've done something that caused pain to someone else.
2. *Honestly admit.* This can be the hardest part, actually standing in front of someone and humbling yourself to admit what you did. But until you make the decision to admit your fault, it cannot be healed.
3. *Ask for forgiveness.* Asking for forgiveness may be the hardest step of all, as you put your ego, pride, and dignity in the hands of another person—especially the one you have wronged. But it is the only way you can truly find release and freedom.
4. *Seek to rectify.* Once you've gone through the process of acknowledging you've failed, then admitting it and asking for forgiveness, the next step is to actually do something to make it right. If you break something, you must be willing to help put it back together.

Below are some ways to ask for forgiveness.

1. *Write a letter/email.* Writing a letter has been and will continue to be one of the best ways to say you're sorry.

It shows you've thought about your actions and actually gone to the trouble to recognize your faults. This will mean a lot to the receiver and is especially appreciated in romantic relationships.

2. *Talk face-to-face.* There is something scary about looking someone in the eyes and admitting fault. But the same thing that makes it scary makes it powerful. When you take a little time to sit down and address your poor actions with seriousness, it shows you care about the pain you've caused.

3. *Bring it to God in prayer.* If your offense is against God, you need only to go before him to be forgiven and set free. If you honestly acknowledge your offense, ask for forgiveness, and seek to rectify it, you will be met with love and grace.

11 A Jester of Joy

In every class, there is a class clown. I was that guy. I loved making people laugh and finding joy in every moment, because laughter is one of the great connectors. But even more than that, finding joy in even the most upsetting situations has given me the strength to take on the battles this life throws at me.

In many ancient kingdoms filled with important roles and positions, one stands out as an odd addition. In the midst of generals, advisors, warriors, and politicians is something that isn't like the others: the jester! Right in the name we see the position was one of lighthearted fun, jokes, and levity, but I think in looking through the consistent appearance of this position (sometimes referred to by different titles) in many cultures and kingdoms, this person might just be more important than previously thought.

For some reason, kings throughout history thought it was important to have a jester as a fixture in the courts. Jesters were tasked with bringing joy, laughter, and happiness to what were often dark times and difficult situations. I can imagine they brought much-needed comfort in moments of deep stress.

We, too, are facing the angst brought about by a broken world. Across our screens and conversations, it seems there is never a shortage of something new and terrible to talk about, worry over, and be upset by. No wonder we still have our own kind of jesters performing as comedians and entertainers. It's no surprise we still are drawn to the things that bring us joy and laughter. We need them.

Being a king is heavy business. It takes effort, grit, and determination. There are wars and tragedy, responsibilities and frustration. And just like the kingdoms of old, our own personal kingdoms and worlds will experience tumultuous moments and sometimes seasons. And while serious minds are important while dealing with real issues, without the ability to find joy, life becomes much harder to bear.

God created us and the world around us beautifully. Over and over again in Scripture, he speaks of the necessity of joy, even in the midst of hard situations. God isn't just the God who gave us morals and theology and lists of rules; he's also the God who laughed, who rode a donkey, and who smiled as the crowds cheered when he entered the city. He's the God who said, "Let the children come to me" (Matt. 19:14).

Let's look to King David, who while in the midst of a life filled with wars, sadness, death, and hurt was found dancing in the street. And while some looked on with disdain, God actually loved seeing David worship him with such joy and blessed him.

There are many reasons to be sad and serious in this world, but we serve the King. We follow a God who desires for us to find joy because he knows we need it. In our own personal kingdoms, we must begin to find our own "jesters," our own places and people that bring us joy so we can better sustain the hardships that will come our way. Maybe it's a friend or an activity, a meal or a show, or simply taking a walk and listening to music that brings a little light back into our world when it has begun to feel dark.

Joy is important. It's not frivolous or something to be discarded. Instead, we should seek joy for both ourselves and those around us. It will not only bring levity to a heavy world but also give us strength to keep going and sharing the story God has for us to tell.

KING'S QUESTIONS

1. Do you think laughter and joy are a part of a healthy life?
2. What makes you laugh? What makes you happy?
3. How can you make room in your life to laugh and find joy even when it's not easy?

Scripture Reading

A cheerful heart is good medicine,
but a broken spirit saps a person's strength.

Proverbs 17:22

KING TIP #11

A List of the Best One-Liners and Short Jokes

Everyone wants to be funny! Because when you are able to make people laugh, you gain their trust and friendship. Laughing brings people together and sheds light in a dark world. Below are a few tried-and-true jokes sure to get the room laughing at your next social gathering!

1. "Never judge someone until you have walked a mile in his shoes. By that time, you will be a mile away from him *and* have his shoes!"
2. "What do William the Conqueror and Winnie the Pooh have in common? Their middle name!"

3. "I haven't slept for three days! You know why? That would be way too long . . ."

4. "People say I am very condescending. You see, that means I talk down to people. Understand now?"

5. "You know what they say about cliff-hangers . . ."

6. "I, for one, like roman numerals."

7. "There are three kinds of people in this world: those who are good at math and those who aren't."

8. "I wondered why the rock kept on getting bigger and bigger. Then it hit me!"

9. "What's the difference between being ignorant and being apathetic? I don't know and I don't care."

10. "Don't you hate it when people ask a question then answer it themselves? I sure do."

The Humble Lord

When we hear the word *king*, a host of images might flood our minds. For me, most often these mental pictures have been pulled from movies, history books, and stories and include gold, power, and physical might. Kings throughout history have been symbols of the peak of what a man can be. They have respect, they are feared, and they have every material thing they desire at their fingertips.

In embracing our position as kings, we may find this picture alluring. Personally, it connects with and promises the fulfillment of all my basic desires and relief from my constant insecurities of inadequacy. But when we look at our Creator, the King of Kings, the One who bestowed this royal crown on our heads, we see a very different picture of what kind of king he has called us to be.

In the beginning of the New Testament, we find the story of the God of the universe stepping down into our world to show us how we were meant to live and who we were meant to be. The King of the universe took on flesh and entered our broken world to bring life. But the way he entered is so very different from the kings the world has created.

Jesus—God in the flesh, Emmanuel—didn't enter the world in fine robes, marching with an army, holding an iron sword; instead, he entered the world as a vulnerable baby, born to a poor couple who placed him not on a gold throne but in a manger of golden hay. In his life on earth, Jesus didn't collect for himself castles and wealth, but instead, he slept on floors and wandered the city streets preaching redemption. This Lord of Lords didn't surround himself with socially popular figures or acquire powerful armies; instead, he spent his time with sinners, prostitutes, the lame, the weak, and the lowly. And, astonishingly, through this humble and backward rule, he changed all of history and brought redemption to the world.

We may be strongly tempted to want the pictures of a king that the world offers us—the ones we see on TV and in magazines who have adoration, popularity, riches, and influence. We live (and have always lived) in an age that tells us to be a true ruler in our world. We must acquire what we want when we want it, if not by the skin of our teeth or the charms of our tongues, then by the edge of a sword.

But this is not the kind of king God has created us to be. This is a counterfeit king who lives only for a fleeting kingdom. We have instead been asked to follow the example of our God, in the life of Jesus, to live for a completely different kind of kingdom and be a completely different kind of king. A ruler who leads with servant leadership and humility and by giving of oneself.

Matthew 19:16–30 tells the story of Jesus offering a rich young ruler a place in the kingdom he is setting up, and the willing ruler inquires what will be asked of him. Jesus tells him he must give all his possessions to the poor, all his earthly trappings for a greater treasure in the kingdom of heaven. Unfortunately, this is too big of an ask for the rich young ruler, and he walks away.

We are all offered a place in the kingdom God is creating, but each of us will be asked to give away the trappings that hold our heart to temporary things. We are asked to take off our opulent robes and instead put on a garment of humility, a garment only true kings will put on. It will be hard and require great sacrifice, but to receive the eternal kingdom God has given us, it will be necessary.

We must ask ourselves what kind of king we will be and what kingdom we are living for. Is it one of temporary pleasures or eternal glory? Will we chase the image the world has given us of what a king should be, complete with riches, fame, and power? Or will we follow the humble but powerful footsteps of Jesus into a kingdom where the last is first, we learn to serve each other, and humility reigns supreme?

The choice is ours.

KING'S QUESTIONS

1. Why should we choose humility in a world that doesn't value it?
2. Practically speaking, why is humility a good thing?
3. What are ways we can begin to practice humility in our own lives?

Scripture Reading

Don't brag about tomorrow,
   since you don't know what the day will bring.

Let someone else praise you, not your own mouth—
   a stranger, not your own lips.

Proverbs 27:1–2

KING TIP #12

The Differences between Confidence and Cockiness

There's a fine line between confidence and cockiness. One helps you find your way in the world, speaks truth to the ones around you, opens doors to your dreams, and allows you agency in your life choices. The other causes unearned pride, makes others feel small, is self-serving, and ultimately separates you from the ones around you. So how do you make sure you don't drift into cockiness while being confident? Knowing the differences between the two will help meet that goal:

1. **Confidence** allows you to compliment and give attention to others because you know your worth and value. **Cockiness** makes you insecurely demand other people's praise and crave attention.

2. **Confidence** is the ability to say what is true even when it's not easy. **Cockiness** has only the ability to say things that will make you look good.

3. **Confidence** is an inner strength that can empower both you and others. **Cockiness** has no intrinsic strength, so it seeks to take strength from others.

4. **Confidence** is knowing your inner worth without having to advertise it in shallow and meaningless ways. **Cockiness** is needing to prove your worth by showy displays of money, status, and material things.

5. **Confidence** can be a powerful and peacemaking presence in tense situations. **Cockiness** will heighten stress by making demands of others.

6. **Confidence** is standing firm even when attacked because you know the truth. **Cockiness** is lashing out at

others out of fear to try to control a narrative and shape perceptions.

7. **Confidence** is the ability to admit a wrong, knowing you are loved no matter what. **Cockiness** means seeking to hide your mistakes and protect your pride by employing dishonest tactics.

8. **Confidence** handles confrontation with kindness. **Cockiness** starts fights.

9. **Confidence** is a peaceful knowledge of who you are. **Cockiness** is a fearful demand to make people think you're something you're not.

10. **Confidence** is founded in the truth of wisdom and reality. **Cockiness** is founded in the lies of pride and ego.

Self-Sacrifice to Live

There's a story that comes from the darkness of the death camps of World War II. A priest was among the prisoners suffering at the hands of their captors, and one day, as a show of perverse power, the prison guards decided to kill ten men by locking them in a bunker and starving them to death over a period of two terrible weeks. Ten men were chosen, and as they were being marched to their deaths, one of the men began pleading with his captors to let him live because he had a wife and children. His pleas fell on deaf ears, except for the priest who had heard the man's cries. The priest stepped to the captors and asked to be put in the man's place, to give his life so the man could live. This priest was a true king.

Because we've been given the vision for what a *true* king looks like from the King of Kings, Jesus, it changes everything about how we are called to live in the domains God has given us. It's a way that isn't tied to the temporal kingdoms of this world and instead will last into eternity.

In the world, we are taught to take what we can, to use others for personal gain, and to get ahead by any means necessary. But God has invited us into the kingdom of heaven and given us another way—a harder way, but a better one. A way of sacrifice.

Jesus says, "There is no greater love than to lay down one's life for one's friends" (John 15:13). This is how we take part in the everlasting kingdom of heaven. We lay down and sacrifice our lives for others, since our King has done this for us.

To the world, sacrifice seems silly. Why would we give up having something we want? Why would we lay down our own life if we only get one? And those questions make sense if you look at this world as the only thing you can get. If we're all just going to die, why wouldn't we take all we could with the limited time we have? There are no ultimate consequences, so we may as well get ours while we can. But in the eternal kingdom of God, we are asked to use this temporary life as one of sacrifice, service, and laying down our lives for others.

This concept goes against everything the world says and our flesh feels. As my mother always said, "Loving, serving, and sacrificing for others isn't natural . . . it's supernatural." And while this way feels so antithetical to the fulfillment we all seek, I propose it's the only way we will ever find true peace in this world. It's the only way we will find life in the next.

But to do this logistically, we don't need to guess how it's done. Jesus, our Creator, the great King, has shown us what living as a true sacrificial king looks like. He showed us what laying down our lives for the inhabitants of our kingdom looks like.

God, knowing we were dead in our mistakes and brokenness, didn't sit back on his throne and scoff at our failings. He didn't stay in the comfort and safety of his castle walls in heaven but instead entered our world, took on our sin, and like the priest in the story, gave his life so we could live. This is the example we are given as to what a true king does. And since the King of Kings has done this for us, we now must do this for others.

We live for an eternal world, one that looks very different from the one we've created here. It's a world of beauty, love, forgiveness, and joy, but we don't inherit this kingdom the way the world inherits theirs. To be a part of the kingdom of heaven, we must learn what self-sacrifice means and act it out. Perhaps it will never be taking another man's place in a death camp, or perhaps it will, but right now, every day we can begin to serve and sacrifice for others in the way God has shown and done for us. We can start by seeking to meet the emotional and physical needs of those around us even when it costs us our time, effort, or money. "For even the Son of Man came not to be served but to serve others and to give his life as a ransom for many" (Mark 10:45). This verse shows what kind of king we are called to be.

KING'S QUESTIONS

1. Do you think self-sacrifice is required to be a good king? Why or why not?
2. What are ways people have sacrificed for you?
3. What are some ways you can sacrifice for others?

Scripture Reading

Imitate God, therefore, in everything you do, because you are his dear children. Live a life filled with love, following the example of Christ. He loved us and offered himself as a sacrifice for us, a pleasing aroma to God.

Ephesians 5:1–2

KING TIP #13

Six Ways to Serve

Service is an important part of becoming a good king. It can be hard to figure out where and how to serve people, but there are many groups and charities that offer the chance to help out and give back in ways you are actually passionate about! Below are six ideas for serving the community and people around you in a practical and effective way.

1. *Aiding a homeless shelter.* Be it serving food in the kitchen or passing out blankets, volunteering at your local homeless shelter will give you a chance to help those less fortunate than you in a real and tangible way.

2. *Conserving nature.* If you love the outdoors and protecting God's creation, there are all sorts of groups dedicated to cleaning parks, carving hiking trails, and protecting wildlife.

3. *Performing arts.* If you have a talent in the arts, a great way to use that gift is to entertain the hospitalized and elderly. Singing a song, doing a magic trick, or telling a joke could be just the thing to brighten someone's day.

4. *Teaching or tutoring.* If you have an education in things that people are seeking to learn, teaching or tutoring someone who doesn't have access to expensive schooling or training might be a perfect way to help them expand their mind and possibilities. Teach an instrument, language, or practical skill!

5. *Calling or meeting with a friend.* Sometimes reaching out to a friend who needs to talk, either in person or on the phone, can make a huge difference. Just listening to someone and being present for them is a huge act of service that will make a big difference.

6. *Doing chores.* Chores aren't just for kids. Helping your parents or neighbor clean their house, mow their lawn, or cook a meal can relieve so much stress for people who need a break and to be shown love.

Serving doesn't just help the ones we are serving; it helps us. Multiple studies have shown how good it is for our brains, minds, emotions, and physical health to help others. So get out there and find your own way to give back. It will do you and the ones you love good.

 # Abdicating
and Reclaiming

There's a famous story I think most of us have heard in one form or another. It's about the son of a nobleman who renounces his name, family, and home; takes his inheritance early; and leaves home to squander his money on prostitutes, parties, and crazy living—only to eventually find himself alone, broke, and homeless as a result of his choices. Realizing how badly he has messed up, he decides to return to his father's land and begs to be a servant in his father's household, thinking there's no way he'd ever be considered a son and heir again after what he has done.

But the twist ending that echoes around the world today is that when the son is still far off, his father sees him in the distance because he's been looking for him day in and day out. Instead of turning him away, shunning, or unleashing his anger on him, the noble father embraces him, cleans him up, dresses him in robes fit for a king, and celebrates. He invites the son back to live not as a servant but as an heir. He offers the son lavish love and grace, not because the son deserves it but because the son is his.

While the story of the prodigal son is a parable, stories throughout history echo the same plot points. Many times, an heir to the throne decided he didn't want to live within the boundaries of the kingdom he was born into and cast off his crown, abdicating the throne for his own personal end.

As I read these stories, I think of how many times I have cast off my own crown—the one God has graciously endowed to me along with the title of heir—and decided to live my own way, with my own rules, to achieve my own desires. When I've done this, I've walked away from God's calling on my life. Like the prodigal son, when we do this we will eventually find ourselves in a mess of our own design and suddenly realize everything we have given up: the inheritance we squandered, the calling we were given, and the position as sons and heirs we cast away so carelessly for cheap pursuits.

At this point we can fall into despair. Perhaps even reading these pages about claiming and living out the God-given royalty in our lives can sting. It hurts to realize that maybe we could have been heirs and rulers with our King, but because of our poor and selfish choices we no longer have a chance at being anything more than a lowly servant in God's kingdom.

But I want to point us back to the end of the story we just read. This story was told to us by our King. I believe in hope for us prodigals—heirs who through our choices have abdicated our thrones to live in our own sad world—and I want us to see that hope. Like the father in the story, God, our Father, is waiting and looking for us. When he sees us approach him again, even though he's fully aware of what we've given up, he will welcome us back with open arms, not so we can be lowly workers but as sons and heirs. He will put our crowns back on and invite us fully into the inheritance and kingdom he has created. This isn't because we deserve it; it's because this is who he is and he loves his children.

So no matter what we have done or where we have been, our King invites us back with open arms to reclaim our positions as kings and heirs in his realm because we are his.

Today is the day. Run home and reclaim your crown. Your gracious Father is waiting.

KING'S QUESTIONS

1. Have you felt like you have wandered away from or given up your calling?
2. Do you believe you can return?
3. What are some areas of calling you can reclaim in your life?

Scripture Reading

Praise the LORD!

I will thank the LORD with all my heart
    as I meet with his godly people.
How amazing are the deeds of the LORD!
    All who delight in him should ponder them.
Everything he does reveals his glory and majesty.
    His righteousness never fails.
He causes us to remember his wonderful works.
    How gracious and merciful is our LORD!
He gives food to those who fear him;
    he always remembers his covenant.
He has shown his great power to his people
    by giving them the lands of other nations.
All he does is just and good,
    and all his commandments are trustworthy.
They are forever true,
    to be obeyed faithfully and with integrity.

He has paid a full ransom for his people.
    He has guaranteed his covenant with them forever.
    What a holy, awe-inspiring name he has!
Fear of the LORD is the foundation of true wisdom.
    All who obey his commandments will grow in wisdom.

Psalm 111

KING TIP #14
Dealing with Debt and Saving Money

While we can be forgiven of all our mistakes by God, life is not always so kind. Dealing with financial missteps can be hard, especially when the debt we carry seems to keep getting heavier. Here are a few tips to begin dealing with debt so it won't be a forever burden we have to bear.

1. *Make a budget.* The start to getting your finances under control is knowing exactly what you are making, then using that metric to inform what you spend. Planning out your month, or even week, financially will give you realistic guidelines to follow and keep you accountable in your spending. There are some great budgeting apps available that might be helpful.

2. *Work at your goal little by little.* It can be tempting to want to just wipe out all your debt or save up lots of money. Then you may get depressed and give up when you can't accomplish that quickly. But don't lose heart. Getting out of debt or building your savings is a process and will take longer than you want (unless you suddenly become filthy rich!). Putting aside just a little bit and/or paying down debt bit by bit every month will be worth it

in the end. While it will take time, you will be glad you invested little by little when you are either out of debt or have solid savings—or both!

3. *Talk to a professional.* There are many great resources from professionals who know what they're talking about that can help you learn how to take care of debt— including hotlines, books, and debt-relief programs. They will tell you how to get lower interest rates, consolidate debt, and even negotiate lower payments. It's always a good idea to talk to someone reputable who also has experience.

4. *Cut out unnecessary spending.* It can be hard to cut back on spending when you've become used to living a certain way. But eliminating some of the less important things in your life can free you up to put more resources toward the important ones. This might mean cutting back on eating out, getting rid of a couple subscription services, or stopping online shopping. It will ultimately become second nature and help keep you stable.

5. *Start spending within your means.* One of the first things to do when dealing with debt is learn how to spend only the money you can afford to spend. When you spend only the amount you have coming in and nothing more, you will be able to get your finances under control.

6. *Get creative and thrifty.* There are great ways to cut back on spending while still getting everything you need. A couple helpful ways to save money but live well is to go to thrift stores for new clothes and household items or practice some awesome recipes at home instead of ordering food from a restaurant.

15 War and Peace

Of the past 3,400 years of recorded human history, only 268 of them have been fully peaceful without wars somewhere on the globe.[1] To some this might be astonishing, but to those who have studied human nature, this will come as no surprise.

When we think about kings and their kingdoms, we usually remember the mighty armies they so often led. We think about the battles they fought and the bloody wars they won and lost. Such a big part of being a king throughout history was stained red. As a boy I fantasized about being one of the knights I read about. I was a mighty warrior who could best many foes and conquer enemies far and near. Imagining myself a hero who stood against darkness and fought evil was good for me. But so often this world has forgotten what is truly worth fighting for. And that, I believe, is peace.

Two thousand years ago we were given a very different kind of King. In places like Rome, rulers of powerful nations carried titles and stories of their might and the death they could inflict on their enemies. Then along came Jesus. He didn't take the titles we so often associate with powerful kings but instead was named the

---

1. Chris Hedges, "What Every Person Should Know about War," *New York Times*, July 6, 2003, https://www.nytimes.com/2003/07/06/books/chapters/what -every-person-should-know-about-war.html.

Prince of Peace—the opposite description from what the world had seen.

Even today, so often we think of the strong as being the ones who hold power and have the ability to physically, mentally, financially, or publicly defeat their enemies. We think of action heroes able to kill a multitude of bad guys, fighters able to destroy their opponents (in either bars or rings), keyboard warriors able to tear apart those they disagree with, and even politicians and rulers who have the ability to overthrow many nations. But the image of a peaceful King that Jesus gave us is as relevant today as it was two thousand years ago.

This picture contrasts with what the world tells us strength is. In fact, it looks like weakness to most of the world. But at the heart of every good king is not war but peace. War brings destruction and death; peace brings prosperity and safety to grow. Fighting brings division and pain; gentleness brings connection and healing. A good king knows the value of these things and seeks at every turn to make them a reality.

Jesus often spoke of how we ought to live in the kingdom of God, saying things like, "If someone slaps you on the right cheek, offer the other cheek also" (Matt. 5:39); "Love your enemies! Pray for those who persecute you!" (v. 44); and "Those who use the sword will die by the sword" (26:52). And while these verses have been used as trite one-liners, I believe instead they are great commands we must learn to live by to become the kings God created us to be.

This isn't about ignoring the power we have. Jesus is King of the world and has the power of the whole universe, but he uses that power to bring about something better than the destruction the world has created. In our own lives, our own realms, we each will feel the desire to fight in one way or another. For some of us maybe it will be the temptation to throw a punch to defend our pride; for others the fight will be on a keyboard, showing our might with our words. But each of us is called to fight to bring peace and healing to our worlds (pun intended). We can use our strength to do it, but we must seek the goal of wholeness for ourselves and others.

Jesus said, "God blesses those who work for peace" (5:9), and in a world that has seen the curses of violence, fighting, and conflict, may we learn to use our strength to bring about a different kind of kingdom—a kingdom of peace.

KING'S QUESTIONS

1. Are you naturally peaceful?
2. What things do you tend to get angry about and fight over?
3. How can we practice being peacemakers in our daily lives?

Scripture Reading

Scoundrels create trouble;
    their words are a destructive blaze.

A troublemaker plants seeds of strife;
    gossip separates the best of friends.

Violent people mislead their companions,
    leading them down a harmful path.

With narrowed eyes, people plot evil;
    with a smirk, they plan their mischief.

Gray hair is a crown of glory;
    it is gained by living a godly life.

Better to be patient than powerful;
    better to have self-control than to conquer a city.

We may throw the dice,
  but the LORD determines how they fall.

Proverbs 16:27–32

KING TIP #15

How to Avoid a Physical Fight and Defend Yourself

In a perfect world, we would never have to physically fight another person. But living in a fallen world where people can be dangerous, selfish, and violent, it is necessary to defend the innocent and sometimes ourselves. We do this never as the attacker but only to pacify a fight. We must not let out aggression or seek revenge. Below are a few self-defense tips to keep you and others—even your attacker—safe.

1. Try at all costs to keep the fight from happening. To do this, use calm tones, nonthreatening language, and understanding statements. Try to find other nonviolent ways to end whatever altercation you find yourself in.
2. If you are able to walk away without you or anyone else getting hurt, do it.
3. If you are attacked, protect your head and face. Keep your hands up and in fists by your jaw and temples, guarding.
4. Drop your chin, keeping your jaw low. This protects your neck and makes your face less of a target.
5. Keep your knees bent, not leaning too far back or forward, to keep your balance and a low center of weight.
6. Stand at an angle to your aggressor. This gives you more mobility and makes you less of a target, and thus harder to damage.

7. Wait to attack. Let them strike first. When they do, seek to knock them off balance.

8. Don't swing big and widely, so as to cause lots of damage. This will take up a lot of energy and usually give them an opening to attack. Instead, make short, direct, quick movements.

9. Aim for the nose, the jaw, or the solar plexus (middle of the stomach); if a hit to one of these nonlethal spots is landed well, it could quickly end the fight.

10. As soon as the assailant is overtaken and subdued and everyone is out of immediate danger, call the authorities and tell them exactly what happened.

11. If the other person has a weapon and running isn't an option, seek to disarm them as quickly as possible. Then immediately dispose of the weapon by throwing it onto a roof, into a locker, or as far as possible.

16   Standing Up Alone

The world is a painful and broken place. We see that there is a force of darkness in the world that Scripture says lives "only to steal and kill and destroy" (John 10:10). We see the reality of this on TV and in the news via pictures of murders and wars, stories about collusion and corruption, and videos of the poor and weak being preyed on. Even in our own lives we see addiction, broken families, abuse, trauma, and so on. Very few people would deny that evil is rearing its ugly head and causing as much destruction and devastation as it can before time is done. But there are also very few who will do anything about it.

In most of the great stories, both fictional and historical, we often find the protagonist of the story is the *one* person, or sometimes multiple people, who decides to do something about the darkness in the world. Be it Frodo, Aslan, the leaders of the civil rights movement, or the martyrs who gave their lives to stand against evil. And for this reason, they are endowed with the label of "hero." So often the heroes of these stories stand almost entirely alone, not because they choose to be alone, but because they are the only ones answering the call of their times.

Darkness is present in all our lives. It might not look like an evil mastermind or the Dark Lord Sauron, but make no mistake—there is darkness in our world. And we have a choice. We can ignore it and hope someone else does something about it, or we can decide, like the heroes did in their stories, to make a difference.

To be the kings God has called us to be, we must be willing to stand up against the darkness of the world even if no one else does. Fighting this darkness will look different for all of us. Perhaps you have noticed the hurting homeless population in your area and decide to help however you can. Perhaps you've seen instances of bullying in your school and you choose to protect someone who can't protect themselves. Or maybe you use your time to join a group that fights sex trafficking, addiction, abuse, or racism.

A good king doesn't ignore things. Instead, he stands against the evil in his kingdom. We must do the same, even if we stand alone.

KING'S QUESTIONS

1. Are you ever scared to stand up for what you know is right? Why?
2. What is something you think someone needs to stand up for?
3. What are a few ways you can practice standing up for what you know is right?

⚜

Scripture Reading

Give justice to the poor and the orphan;
    uphold the rights of the oppressed and the destitute.
Rescue the poor and helpless;
    deliver them from the grasp of evil people.
But these oppressors know nothing;
    they are so ignorant!

They wander about in darkness,
while the whole world is shaken to the core.

Psalm 82:3–5

KING TIP #16

How to Become an Activist

Being an activist has acquired a bad name in recent years. It has become synonymous with throwing public fits and demanding other people do things. But being active in making positive changes in the world is a beautiful thing we should all strive for. So here are a few ways you can stand up to evil and fight for good in your world.

1. Think about the things you or your loved ones have gone through—things that personally affect you and make you sad and that you'd like to see changed.
2. Look around the world and take note of places and ways destructive things are happening, even if they're activities you have participated in. Being aware of what hurts the world is essential to helping it.
3. Research. Before you shout your opinions or share them online, do lots of research, educate yourself, and find the most complete perspective on an issue so you can best help.
4. Think creatively about practical things within your means that you can do to help. You could become a volunteer or create videos, music, or artwork to bring attention to an issue. Or you might write a well-researched and eye-opening article that others can share.
5. Don't get caught up in anger and hate. Learn to promote what you love instead of bashing what you hate.

6. If you have the money to give, give! It especially helps to support people who have experience with a particular issue since they will have the best insight and practices in place to make a difference.

7. Don't feel guilty for not fixing all the world's problems. We all have a responsibility to help in the ways we can. But we won't be able to solve every issue and problem, even if we want to.

8. Have fun. Being active and helpful can seem like a calling that means you have to be angry and serious all the time. But part of what the world needs is people who are happily helping the world. Without joy, you will burn out quickly and perhaps do more harm than good.

9. Make it personal. While joining movements and groups can be a great way to help, simply assisting the people around you—your friends and family members—with their issues can make a world of difference.

The Castle

We've done a lot of talking about what and who kings are, but we haven't spoken about where kings live. Kings live in castles. And the picture in many of our minds is a palace filled with opulent things, fleshly pleasures, and displays of greatness. And while many kings had these things, they were not the heart of what a castle was or why it was built. Castles weren't just a place for the king to display his power and wealth. Castles were built at the highest point in the land and crafted with the highest-quality materials to serve both as a beacon of strength to visitors and a place of protection, prosperity, and life for those inside the kingdom.

Like it has been for thousands of years, the world outside the walls of our kingdom remains chaotic and broken, bent on causing destruction, death, and often just exhaustion. Having phones, cars, and modern comforts, we might think we no longer need castles. And while we no longer need protection from ruthless, sword-swinging armies on horseback, I would argue our hearts, minds, and bodies need a place where we can find protection from the enemies of depression, addiction, loneliness, and tiredness that seek to take us down each day.

To be consistently good, healthy kings, we must create for ourselves a castle—a place of rest and protection where we can return from battle and dress our wounds. A place where we can recharge, train, and invite others in to do the same.

Today, this won't look (usually) like a mighty structure with turrets and thrones, but we can build our castles right where we are—in our studio apartments, basements, dorms, rooms, and houses. We can start seeing our living spaces as more than just places to eat and sleep; instead, they are a place to thrive and find life.

In my little apartment, I like to take time to light candles, fill my kitchen with good and healthy food, surround myself with books, play evocative music, watch inspiring movies, and hang pictures on the walls that bring me joy when my eyes fall on them.

The world is a tiring and unsafe place to live, work, and fight, which makes it all the more necessary to have a life-giving place in which to center ourselves. So maybe today is the day to start seeing your space as not simply a place of survival but rather a place of thriving, protection, healing, and life. Build your castle, kings.

KING'S QUESTIONS

1. Do you think having a dedicated place where we can find peace is important?
2. What places have you experienced like that?
3. How can you create a place like that for yourself?

Scripture Reading

I love you, LORD;
    you are my strength.
The LORD is my rock, my fortress, and my savior;
    my God is my rock, in whom I find protection.
He is my shield, the power that saves me,
    and my place of safety.
I called on the LORD, who is worthy of praise,
    and he saved me from my enemies.

The ropes of death entangled me;
    floods of destruction swept over me.
The grave wrapped its ropes around me;
    death laid a trap in my path.
But in my distress I cried out to the LORD;
    yes, I prayed to my God for help.
He heard me from his sanctuary;
    my cry to him reached his ears.

Psalm 18:1–6

KING TIP #17
Tips on Creating a Castle

Creating a castle, man cave, study, or home to rest, learn, recharge, dream, imagine, pray, and work is essential to thriving in a chaotic world. Below are a few tips on how to turn whatever your space is into something uniquely special and life-giving to you. Even tough guys should know about interior design.

1. *Location.* Deciding where to set up your place is important. It will depend on what you want out of it and what

kind of person you are. Typically, the most effective places are ones you can steal away to—rooms that aren't in the middle of a house or near lots of noise and bother. Basements, corner rooms, or outdoor converted sheds/garages are great choices. This way it can be a peaceful space where you can center yourself mentally and spiritually in solitude but also invite people into when you so desire.

2. *Aesthetic.* Find a look and feel that fits you and your personality. Something that will give you pleasure. If you're an intellect, this might be a place filled with old books, sayings, and darker wood tones. If you're an adventurer or outdoorsman, you might include maps, souvenirs from your quests, and pictures of places you'd like to go, all complemented by earthy tones. For the movie/comic man, this space could include framed posters of favorite comics and movies and curated displays for collectibles in a bright, exciting color palette. Whatever your aesthetic, surround your space with things that bring you joy in a cohesive and consistent look!

3. *Furniture.* Once you have the feel of your space finalized, focus on finding pieces of furniture you will use. If you like movies, find a comfortable couch to view them by yourself or with others on a nice media setup. If you like time alone to read and write, consider large, comfy leather chairs. And if you are a man with many projects, consider a sturdy, well-made wooden desk you can sit behind to better help you accomplish your work. A few pieces of well-thought-out furniture will bring your space together and give you a way to exist in it to the fullest degree.

 Rest

Jesus knew the value of rest. Over and over again, Jesus would finish his work healing the sick, speaking to thousands, or doing miracles, only to disappear to a quiet place of rest. Even back in the Genesis account of the creation, for six days God acted with passion as he created the entire universe, but then God himself carved out a day to rest.

So much about being king has to do with chasing ambition, leading, creating, changing, and acting. But to achieve all these things, we must grasp hold of and take seriously another aspect that doesn't immediately cross our minds when thinking of our duties as kings: *rest*.

Regardless of our power, influence, might, or ability, each of us is a human who is limited. So often the world around us, with all its problems to solve, battles to fight, and competitions to win, can make us think we will fall behind, fail, or miss out if we stop to rest. But in all the hurry and stress the world has to offer, often we end up walking away only with exhaustion and disappointment.

The reality is that as humans we were created to do amazing things in the world. We were made to work hard and to do so much that we get tired. And being tired is a blessing from God. It is a physical, mental, and emotional reminder that we need to recharge. It forces us to stop to breathe and take in the beauty of the world we are trying to change. Rest and quiet are not only important but vital for us to be able to continue the work God has for us.

We don't just climb the mountains to win the peak; we also do it for the view. And to take in the view on the way up, we must sometimes stop along the way and look out over the beauty where we are.

Rest is a vital aspect of ruling well the things God has given us. It will look different for all of us, and it is not passive. Rest is not always just vegging out or turning your mind off. Instead, rest is taking the time to eat a good meal, talk with someone who encourages us, read a book that inspires new ideas, or connect with the One who made us and can renew our strength.

Tired, angry, frustrated, and drained people cannot rule their kingdoms well. But kings who have learned the value of balance will affect their domains with the most positive power. For it's in rest and silence away from the noise and in the presence of God that we rediscover the strength, inspiration, and passion for living out our story. It's in rest that we can again connect with our Creator and be reminded of who we are and what we were created for.

KING'S QUESTIONS

1. Are you good at resting? Why or why not?

2. Do you think rest is important?

3. What are some ways and places you can start practicing rest in your own life?

❧

Scripture Reading

O God, listen to my cry!
  Hear my prayer!
From the ends of the earth,
  I cry to you for help
  when my heart is overwhelmed.
Lead me to the towering rock of safety
  for you are my safe refuge,
  a fortress where my enemies cannot reach me.
Let me live forever in your sanctuary,
  safe beneath the shelter of your wings!

For you have heard my vows, O God.
  You have given me an inheritance reserved for those
    who fear your name.
Add many years to the life of the king!
  May his years span the generations!
May he reign under God's protection forever.
  May your unfailing love and faithfulness watch over
    him.
Then I will sing praises to your name forever
  as I fulfill my vows each day.

Psalm 61

KING TIP #18

Tips on Proactive and Intentional Resting

It can be a hard task to truly rest in this busy and stressful age. Even when people do get time off, they end up letting their rest be mindless—watching hours of TV or playing endless video games.

But mindful resting with the true intention of centering yourself and recharging is a necessary aspect to being a healthy person and living a balanced life. Below are a few tips for how not to waste your free time and find real, useful, centering rest.

1. *Meditate.* Unfortunately, meditation has, through the years, been associated with out-there hippies, when in reality, meditation is something godly men have practiced for centuries. A great way to start meditating is to first find a peaceful place (in nature, a room with a view, or even a closet). Then sit in an upright position, close your eyes, and focus on breathing deeply for about a minute. Then, with no agenda or requests, think about the promises, truths, and realities of God. When your mind wanders, don't get frustrated; instead, pick a phrase that will bring you back to your meditation, like "God loves me." Meditation like this has been shown to have amazingly positive effects on our brains and bodies.

2. *Go outside.* When you're tired, the last thing you might want to do is go anywhere. But when you allow yourself to get out of the chaotic, man-made world and step into God's creation, you will almost always find rejuvenation. You could take a gentle hike through a beautiful forest. Maybe you'll want to sit in a park and just think, or go fishing. Stepping into God's creation will bring you closer to the peace he offers.

3. *Read.* Reading is a way you can let your body rest while stimulating your mind and soul. It doesn't have to be stress-inducing study. Instead, find a book that teaches you things you've been wanting to explore. Or maybe find an enthralling story that can let your imagination run wild. Check out that picture book you enjoy flipping through that brings you peace and joy. Reading is a wonderful way

to allow your body to rest while growing your heart and mind.

4. *Listen to music.* Music has been shown to have a huge positive effect on our bodies and mental health. When you turn on music that ministers to your soul or current life experience (without other distractions like TV or texting), you will probably notice your brain centering itself, allowing you to find peace at least for a few minutes. So go light a candle, lie down, and let beautiful musical notes flow over you and your stress.

19 Important People

Part of being a king in times past was surrounding yourself with powerful and influential people. This metric of importance was evidenced by the money people had, the families they came from, and the power they wielded. Kings would dress in fine clothes, enter towns flaunting their money with their entourages, and attend the finest parties to show the sharp difference between the haves and the have-nots. Mixing of the two classes almost never happened, and when it did, when a royal befriended a peasant, it was scandalous.

We do something similar. The currency of fame, popularity, and importance is no less powerful in our lives than it was in times past. We obsess over celebrities and the lives of the rich and famous. We choose who's cool based on the schools they went to, the job they have, or the clothes they wear. And we use "likes" to determine both our own value and the value of others.

Humans have always had a strong desire to be part of the "in crowd," which leads us to surround ourselves with others who make us look cool, feel like we fit in, and better establish the image we want to portray. But looking at the people God used for great things throughout Scripture, I'm often surprised by how differently he saw people and their worth. God made his priorities clear to

Samuel before the shepherd boy David was anointed: "The LORD does not look at the things people look at. People look at the outward appearance, but the Lord looks at the heart" (1 Sam. 16:7 NIV).

The very people the world rejected were the ones Jesus spent time with and used to establish his eternal kingdom. They weren't always clothed in fine robes but often wore rags and tattered animal skins. They rarely started out with power or influence, and more often than not they were small boys, a man with a stutter (Ex. 4:10–13), or widows who were looked down on (Ruth 1). The followers of Jesus were mainly those on the outskirts of the "in crowd" of society—lowly fishermen, working-class shepherds, despised tax collectors, and shamed prostitutes.

We co-heirs and adopted kings in God's new kingdom were all the outcasts once, but we have all been invited to the royal party. None of us deserve the positions we have; instead, we accept the gift God has given us, and with that we offer others love, respect, and friendship the same way God has loved and respected us.

This isn't always easy, and it sometimes comes with the price of not looking "cool." But to be good kings, we have a duty to invite in the outcasts and love the "uncool." When we realize how much we've been given, this awareness will help us reach out with love to those whom society has deemed undeserving or unworthy.

To be true royals in God's kingdom, we must learn every day to see those around us as equals to ourselves, worthy of the same loving treatment we have been shown. Regardless of how we dress, speak, or look, or what job, education, or family we have, we are all outcasts in need of love. We have been invited into this royal family, and we must do the same for others.

KING'S QUESTIONS

1. Is it hard for you to reach out to those who aren't cool?

2. Have you ever been the one who is not the cool one and had someone reach out to you?

3. How can we practice treating *everyone* with respect?

Scripture Reading

The rich think of their wealth as a strong defense;
 they imagine it to be a high wall of safety.

Haughtiness goes before destruction;
 humility precedes honor.

Spouting off before listening to the facts
 is both shameful and foolish.

The human spirit can endure a sick body,
 but who can bear a crushed spirit?

Intelligent people are always ready to learn.
 Their ears are open for knowledge.

Giving a gift can open doors;
 it gives access to important people!

Proverbs 18:11–16

KING TIP #19

A Short Story about Important People

The Warrior, the Wise Man, and the Peasant

Once upon a time in a kingdom far away, there was a wise, old, good king who had no heirs. The king, realizing his life wouldn't last forever, knew he had to decide who would take over his kingdom after he was gone. So he decided he would throw a grand party in the largest hall of the castle and invite all the willing and suitable successors to meet him face-to-face. The invitations went out, and one by one the powerful warriors; intellectual, wise men; and anyone the king thought worthy of his realm eagerly accepted the king's invitation.

On the day of the party, as each of the invitees readied themselves in their finest robes and armor, preparing their speeches to win over the king, the old, wise king decided to disguise himself as a beggar and sit outside the castle doors so he could better survey the potential candidates.

Garbed in old rags and with dirt stains on his face, the good king sat and waited outside his own castle for the guests to arrive. The first guest to arrive was a mighty warrior and knight sporting shiny armor and a long sword. As the knight waited at the door, the good king spoke to the knight, saying, "Please, sir, could a knight so mighty as you offer me a little help? For I am in danger." The knight, without even a second glance at the king, said, "No, I cannot help you. I am far too busy and have more important things to do." The door to the castle opened, and the knight went on his way.

The next guest to arrive was a famous intellectual thinker and wise man wearing fine robes and holding important scrolls. The king approached the wise man, saying, "Excuse me, fine sir, I am so hoping you can help me." The wise man replied, "Get away from me, beggar! I have far more important things to worry about right now!" The door opened, and the wise man went into the party.

Finally, a peasant approached the door. He wore simple but clean clothes made of modest cloth. In his hand he held a loaf of bread. The disguised king approached him. "Excuse me, I am hungry. Could you help me?" The peasant turned to the king and said, "I don't have much, but here is a loaf of bread made from the wheat in my field. You may have it." The king took the gift, and the peasant went inside to the party.

After many hours of feasting inside the castle hall, the king, now dressed in his royal robes, finally made his entrance. The warrior, the wise man, and the peasant stepped forward to meet the good king. The warrior saluted, the wise man nodded, and the peasant bowed.

The king walked past the warrior and the wise man to the peasant and said, "This is who I have decided will take over my kingdom."

The party gasped with surprise, not understanding. The king turned to the men in front of him. "A good king gives what he has to help those in need, be that power, wisdom, or bread." He looked at the peasant. "You gave all you had, caring not for my worldly position but only for my well-being, so to you I give my kingdom." He placed a crown on the peasant's head.

The warrior and the wise man were sent away.

20 The Age and Reign of Men

We live in a modern world that daily seeks to convince us we will live forever. Tied up in commercial taglines, pop songs, and marketing ploys are the messages of "Live for today, don't think about tomorrow," "No regrets," and "Forever young." Behind these words is a desire to lull us into complacency—to keep us distracted enough by pleasure that we don't think too hard about our impending ends.

But as we step back and gaze at the span of history, with all its figures, empires, and happenings, we see how short our time here really is. Great nations have risen and fallen in the course of a history-book sentence. Kings that lived and died exist now only in painted renderings, to be quickly forgotten and replaced. Historical figures and their deeds are often no more than one-word answers on school tests.

In Psalm 144:4, the psalmist compares our lives to a breath of air or a passing shadow. Life is short—very short. We are here today and gone tomorrow. And what we do with the short number of days given to us will determine the legacy we leave behind.

Realizing the briefness of life can be hard and depressing. For some it causes despair, convincing them we face a pointless existence that's just going to end anyway. But the brevity of life can be powerful and inspiring if instead we believe that our souls are part of an endless righteous kingdom. The world encourages us not to think about tomorrow or the future, but to be a good king and leave a meaningful legacy, we must grasp how limited our time is here on earth.

When we put our lives into this context, we will begin to see every choice we make as being infinitely more important. When we allow our minds to rise above the noise and grasp the difficult vision of our ever-approaching end, we just might start to let go of the small and meaningless things we chase and replace them with more worthy and long-lasting pursuits—pursuits that will leave echoes of goodness long after we're gone.

I have wasted many hours in my life. I wish I had something to blame aside from my addiction to comfort and laziness. But the number of times I have played video games or watched mindless TV for uncountable hours is staggering. And sometimes in the middle of what I feel is a well-earned "binge," I think of all the beautiful things I might have created or been a part of with the time I have given away so thoughtlessly.

At this point, I have learned not to let my realizations be an indictment against myself. That choice is too often followed by shame and hopelessness that keeps me in a pointless cycle. Instead, I let the realization of the short amount of time I have here inspire me to do something beautiful. Something that will leave behind traces of goodness in the world long after I leave.

I once heard a preacher say, "I want to die tired, with no more life left in me." This sentence reminds me to spend my days well, as well as I can. I have all eternity waiting to rest in my Creator's presence.

Our time is restricted, and any limited thing is often made more valuable by its own scarcity. So let's learn to prize our time here, use our days well, and aim to leave behind something that might just echo into eternity.

KING'S QUESTIONS

1. Do you live with the feeling of time being limited and important? Why or why not?
2. What are the benefits of valuing the limited time we have?
3. When you consider how to wisely use your time, which activities do you need to prioritize? Are there any activities you need to abandon?

Scripture Reading

Don't put it off; do it now!
    Don't rest until you do.
Save yourself like a gazelle escaping from a hunter,
    like a bird fleeing from a net.

Take a lesson from the ants, you lazybones.
    Learn from their ways and become wise!
Though they have no prince
    or governor or ruler to make them work,
they labor hard all summer,
    gathering food for the winter.
But you, lazybones, how long will you sleep?
    When will you wake up?
A little extra sleep, a little more slumber,
    a little folding of the hands to rest—
then poverty will pounce on you like a bandit;
    scarcity will attack you like an armed robber.

Proverbs 6:4–11

KING TIP #20

A Daily Checklist for Using Your Time Well

Schedules can seem like a good idea when you're trying to use your days well, but often they create more stress and unwanted pressure when you cannot live inside their boundaries. Instead, try a daily checklist! It will help you set goals while allowing you to decide as your day goes on when you will engage with each thing. Below is a daily checklist that will help guide and grow you in important areas every day if you dedicate yourself to it.

Mind

1. ___ Read one chapter of nonfiction literature.

2. ___ Read one chapter of a fiction book.

3. ___ Listen to one podcast, lecture, or sermon.

Body

1. ___ Work out or get some kind of physical activity for twenty minutes.

2. ___ Eat three healthy, balanced meals. (Enjoy one splurge meal a week.)

3. ___ Drink eight glasses of water.

Soul

1. ___ Read one passage of Scripture.

2. ___ Pray for ten minutes.

3. ___ Meditate for ten minutes.

Dreams/Calling

1. ___ Spend one hour on your own creative project or intellectual passion.

2. ___ Write to one person or group that might help you further your dreams.

3. ___ Spend one hour just dreaming about what you want to do and where you want to be.

The checklist above might need to be edited to apply specifically to your life. But each of these areas, when you dedicate yourself to them daily, will result in your overall growth as a person. You will find large returns over time in the small, faithful choices and practices you engage with daily. Hopefully these can give you guidance and structure as you try to use the time you've been given well!

Body of a God

Recently I've watched a multitude of movies about kings, from King Arthur to Thor. In my watching, I've noticed a glaring difference between me and the actors who portray royalty on-screen. No, it's not the swords and magic they use or the grand foes they fight, but instead I've noted their bodies. Most times, they're muscular, toned, and full-abbed. Since our culture seems to worship bodies, putting only the perfect specimens in movies and on magazine covers, I started wondering what importance our bodies have to the concept of ruling ourselves well.

I think most men tend toward one extreme or another. One extreme fully buys into the need to have a "perfect body" in order to be valued by society. The second group, realizing they will never achieve the unrealistic depictions seen on-screen, bitterly rejects the notion of health or its importance and carries on with unhealthy habits.

I have shifted between these places through most of my life. But I think perhaps there is a different option. Maybe we can look at our bodies and health with a new lens that doesn't involve unrealistic, obsessive standards from the world or the bitterness and lethargy that many of us live with.

Throughout history, there have been those who see the body as the ultimate and most important thing about us as humans. If you wander through any museum with statues from the ancient Greek and Roman worlds, you will quickly feel just as insecure as you would looking at the cover of a modern workout magazine. But others saw bodies as evil and the root of everything bad in us. They were things to be hated and even hurt.

In Scripture we see what the true purpose of our bodies is, and with that the importance of our health. Scripture tells us that God created our bodies and said they were "good." It's clear from the earliest words in the Bible that our bodies are good and beautiful things, created by a Master Craftsman to house our souls. Scripture then details that we have useful purposes for our bodies, to "be fruitful and multiply," to "fill the earth and govern it," and to "reign over the fish in the sea, the birds in the sky, and all the animals that scurry along the ground" (Gen. 1:28).

We see that from the very beginning God purposed us to reign, and the beautiful tool he gave us for reigning was our bodies. This perspective might just give us a new vision for how we ought to use and treat our bodies. If God granted us a world to reign over well, we must take care of the tools he has given us to do that with. God assigned us each a specific calling that will require different abilities, some more physical and others more mental, but no matter what our calling is, we have a responsibility to take care of our bodies so they can be used well for the work he intends us to complete. In Ephesians 2:10, Paul reminds us, "For we are God's masterpiece. He has created us anew in Christ Jesus, so we can do the good things he planned for us long ago."

We need not worry about the obsession with bodies that the world has or the indifference we can so often have. Instead, we can begin to see our bodies as houses for our souls and minds. We must take care of them to the best of our ability to continue to serve the kingdoms he has put in our care.

Since Eden, the world has become a more broken and painful place, and the reality is that our bodies will never be perfect on this earth, with its diseases, accidents, and aging. But as we accept the title of kings that *the* King has given us, we can take responsibility for the bodies we have been given, knowing they are designed to help us in our kingdom-building work. And we can find hope in the truth that someday God will make each of us new in a body that will never decay.

KING'S QUESTIONS

1. Do you think taking care of your body is an important part of your work? Why or why not?
2. Do you feel like you are taking care of your body?
3. What are a couple of ways you could invest in your physical health?

Scripture Reading

Don't you realize that your body is the temple of the Holy Spirit, who lives in you and was given to you by God? You do not belong to yourself, for God bought you with a high price. So you must honor God with your body.

1 Corinthians 6:19–20

KING TIP #21

A Healthy and Complete "Super Stew" Recipe

How to Make a Great Gourmet Stew

Having a few recipes in the arsenal, especially ones that look harder than they are, fill you up while looking fancy, are cost-effective, and most importantly, are healthy, is an essential part of being a well-rounded man. The Super Stew is something I have found surprisingly filling, tasty, and nutritious. Here is the recipe!

What you'll need:
1 lb. ground meat
1 onion, chopped
1 c. brown rice
32 oz. chicken stock
1 can diced tomatoes
1 can black beans
1 can white corn
Seasonings to taste
Sour cream
Shredded cheese

Directions:
Sauté the meat with your chopped onion in a large pot in some olive oil. Once cooked thoroughly, dump in the chicken stock and rice, along with the cans of tomatoes, beans, and corn.

Flavor with your favorite seasoning. (I like it spicy, so I suggest cayenne pepper, garlic powder, salt, and pepper.)

Cover the pot and cook for forty minutes on medium-to-low heat, stirring occasionally. The time the stew spends simmering will combine all the flavors and ingredients nicely. If the chicken stock has boiled down and you prefer a soupier texture, add a cup of water with a pinch of salt.

Serve hot with a dollop of sour cream and a sprinkle of shredded cheese and eat up!

The Crying King

The Psalms, written in part by King David, are an interesting addition to the Scriptures, which up until that time had mostly been history, stories, genealogies, and lists of religious procedures. But then we find a book written by a mighty king known for his fighting ability and strength that is filled with deeply emotional words, gut-wrenching lyrics, and desperate cries.

Often we are prone to attach the phrase *stoic strength* to our view of men, especially kings. Most of us have heard the phrase "men don't cry." And many of us run from the uncomfortable emotions that come with addressing the broken, painful, and downright sad things in the world and in ourselves.

It's no wonder we kings tend to hide our sadness, heartache, and other emotions from the world. It's often the world that has caused the grief we feel. Kings live with the pressure to look strong, keep it all together, and grit our teeth through pain. But perhaps we were never meant to listen to the world in the first place on matters of the heart.

So, what a unique thing to find a king, a strong and masculine one at that, so in touch with his emotions that he actually writes them down in heartbreaking poetry for the world to see.

In the New Testament, we find another crying king. The shortest verse in the entire Bible, found in John 11:35, simply says, "Jesus wept." I don't think this verse is an accident. Instead, I think it's a powerful picture that shows how the King and Creator of the universe shed tears, felt pain, and let his emotions be known. Perhaps acknowledging this will free us to follow in his steps and fully express the pain we feel, knowing we are in good company.

The world is a broken place. Each one of us will feel deep pain, and we must do something with it. For so many of us, the answer has been to push it down, ignore it, or let it out in harmful ways that hurt ourselves or others. But perhaps if we can allow ourselves to fully feel and express our pain like Jesus did, we'll start to find healing in the midst of it. Openly communicating our heartache both expels the destructive power it might have had over us and encourages others to connect with us in similar ways.

I daily fight with the notion that I must look strong, keep a stiff upper lip, and never show my weakness in the form of crying. But I'm also learning that if pain is something the greatest King experienced and expressed, perhaps I can too. And perhaps in expressing my feelings, I will find the healing I need. The escape I sought has served only to hurt me and the ones I love.

To be good kings, we must be strong. But maybe, like both David and Jesus, part of being a good, strong king is allowing our bodies, minds, and hearts to express the pain we each feel. Then we can begin to see our own brokenness begin to mend.

KING'S QUESTIONS

1. Do you ever feel pressure to hold it all together and not show emotion? When?

2. How do you think holding in your emotions can affect you?

3. What are ways you can learn to healthfully process the deep emotions you have?

Scripture Reading

O Lord, hear me as I pray;
    pay attention to my groaning.
Listen to my cry for help, my King and my God,
    for I pray to no one but you.
Listen to my voice in the morning, Lord.
    Each morning I bring my requests to you and wait
      expectantly.

Psalm 5:1-3

KING TIP #22

The Five Stages of Grief

Psychologists have found that when humans experience a loss, we almost always enter a process of five stages of grief. Each stage is an important part of processing the loss, but they may not be experienced in this order. Below is an outline of the stages and some ways to deal with each one.

1. *Denial.* So often our first reaction to deep pain and sadness is not to acknowledge it at all. How many times when you were going through something have you told a friend you're fine, when both of you know you are most certainly not? We must address this by learning to accept the

difficulty in our life and not being ashamed or afraid of the pain it has caused. We can't stop the pain of a cut until we admit we are bleeding. The same goes for our minds, hearts, and souls.

2. *Anger.* After acknowledging the loss, often we find ourselves angry about it. We are mad it happened, and we look for people and things to blame—even ourselves. We want to lash out when we finally begin experiencing the hurt. This reaction is natural, but if we stay here, we risk continuing to hurt ourselves and others. One key to moving through this stage is finding a safe outlet for the anger. Maybe it's a physical activity, like boxing or working out, or maybe it's venting to a friend. We can't ignore our anger, but we can control it and find a healthy way to express it.

3. *Bargaining.* At this point we try to make sense of all we've been through and find ways to make it okay. We bargain with reality (or God) and say, "I'll do this if this happens," hoping we can work out a deal. During this time, it's important to have honest and kind voices from wise and caring people speaking into your experience.

4. *Depression.* This is a hard stage, and many people spend a lot of time, sometimes years, here. Depression comes when we feel there's very little to be done, we don't have the energy to fight anymore, and hopelessness sets in. It can be tempting to stay here. But when you're at this stage, you're so close to reaching hope, so don't give up. That's the key—don't give up.

5. *Acceptance.* This is both the end and the hardest place to reach when dealing with life's trauma. It takes intentionality and energy to get ourselves here. But in acceptance, there's peace. We have reconciled in our minds and hearts the hurt that we've experienced, we have

allowed it to grow us, and we have found a way to allow it to be used in the story God is telling. Here we will find redemption and hope for the future, one where the pain of yesterday is transformed into a story of victory for tomorrow.

Kingdom Treasures

Scripture says the love of money is "the root of all kinds of evil" (1 Tim. 6:10), which is a harsh truth evidenced by the greed, abuse, and corruption we've seen so often today and throughout history.

We live in a world that worships the pursuit of money and gives special treatment to those who have it, which can understandably create in us a desire for it and what comes along with it. As we have seen in history, kings were often known for their wealth, including majestic castles with rooms filled with gold and caches of jewels. With money comes power, and it might seem that since we are kings this is a worthwhile pursuit for us. But we've also seen that many destructive things can come along with money, so it would behoove us to find out how we should approach it.

There's a story in the Bible (see Matt. 19:16–30; Mark 10:17–31; and Luke 18:18–30) where a rich young ruler comes to Jesus with a desire for eternal life. Jesus tells the man that to follow him, he must give away all his money to the poor and walk away from his life of privilege. Reading this both now and in years past has been a stinging reminder of how very different God's priorities are from mine and the world's.

In this story, Jesus isn't trying to make the young man hate money. Rather, Jesus is testing him to see where the man's heart truly lies. The young man had all the intentions of being a good person and following Jesus—as long as it was on his own terms and didn't cost him his wealth and what came with it.

I don't think this story is so much an indictment of money as it is a chance to survey our hearts to see what our ultimate priorities are. Money in and of itself isn't a bad thing, but what we do to get it and what we do with it can be.

Money is a tool, that's all—nothing more, nothing less. But when we make it into our god, when we spend our lives worshiping at the foot of its altar, we live wasted lives.

Jesus said, "Where your treasure is, there the desires of your heart will also be" (Matt. 6:21), which leads me to believe that God is more concerned about the position of our hearts than he is the number in our bank accounts.

So how, as kings in God's kingdom, ought we to look at money? Well, I suggest we look at it as a helpful aid we can use for good in service to God's kingdom and nothing more. It's not an identity to show off or an idol to worship. In this world, many people worship the love of money; as true kings, we must learn to test our hearts and see where our true treasure lies. Do we put too much trust in our finances? Do we use it as a way to buy relationships or status? Do we hoard whatever wealth we have instead of giving to those in need? Whether we have millions or minuses in our bank accounts has no bearing on our value to God. Our and others' objective worth has nothing to do with how much money we have.

For years my parents taught me a simple way to be faithful and unattached to the money I receive for my work in this world: give the first 10 percent away. Tithing is a simple way to remind ourselves that whatever we have isn't ours and is to be used in the service of God.

Let us kings ask ourselves where our true treasure lies, what we value, and what we are doing with the things we've been given.

Let us worship the Gift Giver, not the gifts. And remember that where your treasure is, there the desires of your heart will also be.

KING'S QUESTIONS

1. Are you ever tempted to find your worth in material things or status?
2. If you're honest, where does your treasure lie?
3. How can you begin to let go of valuing things like the world does?

Scripture Reading

Why should I fear when trouble comes,
    when enemies surround me?
They trust in their wealth
    and boast of great riches.
Yet they cannot redeem themselves from death
    by paying a ransom to God.
Redemption does not come so easily,
    for no one can ever pay enough
to live forever
    and never see the grave.

Those who are wise must finally die,
    just like the foolish and senseless,
    leaving all their wealth behind.
The grave is their eternal home,
    where they will stay forever.
They may name their estates after themselves,
    but their fame will not last.
    They will die, just like animals.

This is the fate of fools,
though they are remembered as being wise.

Psalm 49:5–13

KING TIP #23

Four Ways to Use Your Money Well

Sometimes it can feel like the entire world is built around just getting more money. And often when someone actually does discover, earn, or win riches, they don't know what to do with it and quickly squander it. A high percentage of lottery winners lose their money within a few years. So wherever you are, how can you use the money you have well? Below are a few tips on how to better the world, yourself, and the ones around you with what you have.

1. *Give.* Learning to give a percentage of everything you make will not only help you avoid creating an idol of or identity from your money, it will also enable you to help those who have less than you. Even just tithing/donating 10 percent of your income can make a world of difference in someone else's life and help you cultivate a heart for helping others in need.
2. *Save.* The very first and simplest way to use your money well is to learn to save it. It can feel like money in hand is meant to be spent, but when you learn to regularly put away what you earn, you are preparing for your future. You never know what life will bring, and to have an ever-growing stash can be of much help in unforeseen times.
3. *Invest.* If done well, investing can be a life-changing practice. When you put your money in places that have the potential to grow it over time, you increase not only your wallet but also your wisdom, patience, and insight.

4. *Spend.* Spending isn't something you'll often find on lists of wise things to do with your money (for good reason). Besides the money you spend on necessities, it's important to learn not to waste your funds on cheap thrills and material things that will soon break but instead to use your money for things that truly matter—things that teach, inspire, heal, and bring joy. Taking a master class, traveling to a new place, sharing a gourmet meal, or experiencing a moving concert are all good examples.

Money is a complicated thing, and the love of it can be "the root of all kinds of evil," but as you become a wiser person, you can also learn how to better use your money for good.

Playing Pretend

As a kid, I spent countless hours in my backyard playing make-believe. I'd usually establish myself as the central figure of whatever fantasy movie, epic book, or adventure game I had most recently come across. I would create imaginary worlds that came to life around me. Box forts became castles, sticks became swords, and boys became heroes. I am sure many of us had experiences and memories like this growing up. I think there's something built into the soul of a child that makes them want to pretend.

As grown men, kings who are all about our important grown-up business in the world, sometimes we look back with condescension at our younger selves. We picture how silly we must have appeared bounding around in plastic armor, swinging our wooden swords. We can think of how much more mature we are now, how much more advanced and adult we are. But I wonder if, as we emulated the heroes we saw on the screen and read about in the pages of our books, we were practicing instead of actually being the heroes of the stories God's given us.

Stories are powerful and important. Stories and our connection to them are woven into the very fabric of the human soul. And I believe stories aren't things we were meant to enjoy only as children and then cast off. Instead, they are the very things that usher us to become the men and kings we are supposed to be. In stories, we don't just find abstract characters; instead, we find ourselves. We learn how normal people become heroes and how we ought to act to be the good guy in the story our own lives are telling.

We often come across the sentiment that to be real grown-ups, we must rid ourselves of fantasy and tale and focus only on real-life problems. But what if stories are the conduit for how we discover for ourselves the identities that will ultimately shape the real world into a brighter and better place? What if all the hours we spent imagining ourselves as kings and heroes prepare us to rule well and heroically, right inside our very reality?

We must engage with stories that inspire us to live as the protagonists we were created to be inside of the story that God is writing. So many of the stories being told today reflect hardened, angry, selfish, and destructive emotions and actions, creating a vicious cycle and inspiring more of the same in the souls of those who ingest them. But when we search for stories that reflect truth, hope, love, and sacrifice, we find that we will slowly begin to reflect the characters who display those strong characteristics.

As kings, we must never stop playing pretend. We must never stop engaging with good and beautiful stories. As we do, we'll find ourselves more naturally living the roles of the good and strong kings God made us to be.

So pick up those books, turn on those movies, and play those games—the ones that give you a world in which heroes live.

KING'S QUESTIONS

1. Have you ever considered how your games, movies, books, and stories affect you?
2. Do you think stories have the power to change or inspire you? If so, how?
3. What kind of stories inspire you? Why?

Scripture Reading

Let this be recorded for future generations,
  so that a people not yet born will praise the LORD.
Tell them the LORD looked down
  from his heavenly sanctuary.
He looked down to earth from heaven
  to hear the groans of the prisoners,
  to release those condemned to die.
And so the LORD's fame will be celebrated in Zion,
  his praises in Jerusalem,
when multitudes gather together
  and kingdoms come to worship the Lord.

Psalm 102:18–22

KING TIP #24

How to Write a Good Story with the Three-Act Structure

For all the novelists, scriptwriters, and other storytellers, learning some basic story structure can help to craft a tale worth telling. The three acts below can be found in almost every single great narrative ever told. Learning this simple but effective form provides the basis for telling and writing beautiful epic stories that capture the hearts and minds of those who listen to and read them.

Beginning. The first act of any great narrative introduces you to the characters—who they are, what they're like, and what they want. This is also the time to present the world the characters live in and the rules that exist in that sphere. Whether Middle-earth, Narnia, or Avonlea, you must welcome the reader/watcher/listener to the location of your story. After establishing the main characters and the world they inhabit, the next thing you reveal is the *inciting incident*, the thing that kick-starts your story. The inciting incident is the plane crash, the murder, the getting or losing the job, the meeting of the girl. This event is important because it leads the reader to the end of your first act, presents the main conflict, and ultimately is the thing that gives your story meaning. In other words, the struggle brought on by the inciting incident is the obstacle your hero must overcome.

Middle. The middle of any story is where the meat is. It's here that all the action ramps up. Every scene builds on the last, with more and more things happening. The reader spends the majority of the story here. You get to see the hero live in a more and more exciting story as the plot progresses. Throughout this act, the action rises and rises and gives birth to twists and betrayals, discoveries and realizations, and eventually you have your victorious climax! Which leads to the last act.

End. It's here in the final third of your story, after all the action, after the victory, that you wrap up all the loose ends. The hero reflects on the lessons they've learned, and you see how the world you were first introduced to has changed. You find what you naturally want from stories: resolution. Resolution helps the protagonist make sense of everything they've been through. The end brings a wholeness to the story you're telling. The lead character will have changed, they will have learned, and they will have retained scars, but they will also hold victory in their heart.

Every good story is unique in style and detail. But at the heart of every good story is a solid structure. Even your own. Hopefully, this guide will be a gentle help as you craft your own tale.

In the Secret Place

Much of what we know about particular kings, both ancient and modern, is from the public persona they offer us. In the old times, kings were often seen on their thrones and on stages in front of eager crowds. Their decrees were announced in the town square and their doings written of in papers. Now we see the rulers of the world on our screens, their faces and actions broadcast to millions. But behind every public face is a private person who lives the majority of their life behind closed doors. We see only a glimpse of who they really are, an incomplete picture, so we don't know the person who exists when the TV shuts off.

In reality, this is true of all of us. Perhaps our audiences aren't as big as the royals on-screen, but still, every day—be it on social media, in a meeting, or behind a pulpit—we give only parts of ourselves to the outside world. The truth of who we really are lies not in the incomplete vision we cast for others to see but in the private man behind the curtain of public life.

Often we hope that small sliver of the person we offer people publicly will be true of the whole of us—that the interesting person we are for an hour with friends is who we really are. But who we really are is reflected by the hours we spend in secret.

While it can feel good to be praised for our public deeds, words, and actions, ultimately, this praise is hollow if beneath it lie inconsistencies. Many stories have been told both now and in ages past about seemingly good people who hid darker lives. Only they and God could see the full truth of who they were, but the signs were there nonetheless. Stories of moral pastors hiding sexual addiction, good politicians hiding selfish corruption, and peaceful-looking husbands and fathers hiding violent tendencies are all too common in the story of mankind.

In a world that worships public image and mercilessly punishes mistakes, we may be tempted to craft a better social appearance and a tighter cell for our darkness to dwell away from the painful light of public scrutiny. But in doing this, we split the whole of who we were created to be, and eventually we will reap the consequences in one way or another. God will forgive us, but reality won't.

So what must we do? Jesus gave a vision that counteracts the world's way of doing things. God, knowing how humanity works, told us, "People judge by outward appearance, but the LORD looks at the heart" (1 Sam. 16:7). In saying this, I believe God sought to remind us that he is far less concerned with our public face than he is with our inward lives. How we act when no one is around, the choices we make when we are alone, and the secret thoughts we have reflect who we really are. It's not the fragile persona we offer to the world.

Jesus was most often upset not by the obvious sinners surrounding him but instead by the Pharisees, who paraded their good works and polished religious veneers while hiding their contaminated hearts. Jesus was concerned not with their public appearance of righteousness but instead with the hidden condition of their hearts.

It's tempting to focus our energy on looking good for the world, but to become the kings we ought to be, we must shift our attention to living a life of goodness in secret where only God can see us. To make good choices when no one is watching. To build character in the absence of praise. To work through our fears and failures privately with God rather than donning a mask. Then—regardless of how we fare in the court of public opinion—the favor of God will be with us.

KING'S QUESTIONS

1. Do you think doing the right thing when nobody's watching is important? Why?
2. Does your visibility change your actions? If so, how?
3. Do you believe God will bless you when you do the right thing in secret? How so?

Scripture Reading

The king's heart is like a stream of water directed by the
Lord;
    he guides it wherever he pleases.

People may be right in their own eyes,
    but the Lord examines their heart.

The Lord is more pleased when we do what is right and
just
    than when we offer him sacrifices.

Haughty eyes, a proud heart,
    and evil actions are all sin.

Good planning and hard work lead to prosperity,
    but hasty shortcuts lead to poverty.

Wealth created by a lying tongue
    is a vanishing mist and a deadly trap.

The violence of the wicked sweeps them away,
because they refuse to do what is just.

The guilty walk a crooked path;
the innocent travel a straight road.

Proverbs 21:1–8

KING TIP #25

Kicking a Bad Habit or Breaking an Addiction

We all have secret sins, habits, and addictions that have harmful effects on our lives. Lust, porn, disordered eating, substance abuse, anger, lying, and stealing are just a few of the things we might struggle with in secret. Below are some steps to begin the journey of kicking that habit and living the life you want to have.

1. *Admit it.* To actually address a bad habit or addiction, you must admit you have one. You can't get help or start fixing what's wrong if you can't admit there's anything wrong.
2. *Tell someone.* You might feel the pressure to handle your struggles all on your own. To fix yourself before anyone sees. But the best way to tackle any major problem is to let wise, caring, helpful people in to support you in your recovery. That could be a close friend, a pastor, a professional therapist, or parent.
3. *Be kind to yourself.* You may be inclined to punish yourself for your behavior, get down on who you are, or engage in self-loathing. While this might feel like the right response, it will actually put you in an unhealthy cycle that will make healing more difficult. Give yourself grace,

knowing that *everyone* has their own battles and struggling with bad habits and addictions is part of the human experience.

4. *Make a plan.* While just gritting your teeth and going cold turkey might work in the movies, in real life, you need to have a plan. And this will look different for each struggle. But when you join programs, set goals, and give yourself things to reach for and boundaries to live within, you are setting yourself up for success.

5. *Don't just run from, run toward.* You may become so focused on getting something out of your life that you forget you also need to be putting something in. With every bad habit you are seeking to get rid of, find a good one to replace it with. It's important not to leave a void but instead to fill your life with healthy, mentally stimulating things (for example, drawing, reading, crafting, or playing sports) to replace the destructive ones.

6. *Rest and reward yourself.* When you spend lots of effort on beating your addiction, you may forget to enjoy the success you've found so far. If you don't slow down from time to time, you will wear yourself out and won't be able to cross the finish line. Take a break and enjoy the view; you've earned it.

7. *Prepare for the long run.* When you finally overcome a habit, you may feel pressure never to mess up again. But the reality is, as long as you live in a broken world with imperfect bodies and minds, you are going to struggle. If you find yourself wrestling again with an old habit, don't despair; take joy in the fact that you beat it once, and you can do it again.

26 More Than We Can Handle

In the middle of the largest city in the US, there is a statue of a bronzed and chiseled man hunched over, muscles bulging, as he carries a globe on his back. This image of Atlas quite literally depicts a man carrying the weight of the world on his shoulders.

Many people, when they hear that phrase or see figures like this one, think it's inspiring. I certainly connect to the desire to carry all the burdens of the world with my own might, to figure it out on my own, and to handle all life throws at me with unmatched strength—emerging victorious as a result of my great power.

In thinking about kings, we often reflect on their power and might. We consider all the strength they have over their foes and troubles. We think of all the influence they have at their disposal and the influence they can exert in any problematic situation that arises.

Perhaps that's the inclination for many of us—to think we must conquer every battle with our own might and strength. There's even an expectation that we will be self-sufficient and hold the ability to rise above any and every problem in this world.

There's an old saying, "God will never give you more than you can handle." Many of us believe this to be a true and good statement. I did. But my belief in the truth of this quote began to fade in the years I regularly found myself overwhelmed with life's trials. Like an outnumbered warrior swinging wildly, I tried my best to "handle" what God had given me, until I eventually came tired, bloodied, and breathless to the realization that perhaps God didn't give me more than I could handle, but life did. And I was not strong enough to endure it all.

But the realization that my might was never going to be enough was actually the conduit for me to discover what a wonderful thing it was to admit I couldn't handle everything on my own. When I acknowledged that my strength was not enough, I found that God was.

Confessing our weakness and inability offers us a chance to rely on God's strength and competence. Humbling ourselves enough to say, "I can't do this on my own," means accepting God's offer to fight alongside us. It can be hard to admit that life is bigger than us, that there are moments we cannot handle ourselves, weights our backs cannot bear, and fights our strength cannot win. But there is comfort, peace, and victory when we discover we don't have to, and in fact, were never meant to. God was. When we accept that we are not strong enough to defeat the hordes of enemies that take the form of depression, addiction, job loss, tragedy, and loneliness by ourselves, we will find the relief that comes from realizing he will fight our battles with us and share the weight of the world.

Every time we admit we cannot do it on our own, we accept the invitation to draw closer to the King who can.

KING'S QUESTIONS

1. Do you feel strong enough to handle all life's problems? What gives you this strength?

2. What do you do when you feel weary or weak?

3. Have you ever taken an opportunity to lean on God when you feel overwhelmed? If so, when?

Scripture Reading

But I will call on God,
  and the LORD will rescue me.
Morning, noon, and night
  I cry out in my distress,
  and the LORD hears my voice.
He ransoms me and keeps me safe
  from the battle waged against me,
  though many still oppose me.
God, who has ruled forever,
  will hear me and humble them.
For my enemies refuse to change their ways;
  they do not fear God.

As for my companion, he betrayed his friends;
  he broke his promises.
His words are as smooth as butter,
  but in his heart is war.
His words are as soothing as lotion,
  but underneath are daggers!

Give your burdens to the LORD,
  and he will take care of you.
  He will not permit the godly to slip and fall.

Psalm 55:16–22

KING TIP #26

Three Reasons to Go to Therapy

Therapy can be a scary thing to talk about. It's loaded with misconceptions and might even make you feel weak by accepting you need it. But it's something *everyone* needs in their life at some point. In the same way you see the doctor for your body, you need help for your mind and heart. It is a strong act to admit need and choose to get help. Below are three good reasons why you should try therapy.

1. *You get a third-party perspective.* It can be helpful to counsel yourself either through thoughts or education, and it can also be helpful to have family and trusted friends give you advice and input. But a counselor offers something neither your mind nor your friends and family can: a completely unbiased perspective. When meeting with a therapist, you will get honest opinions and educated insight that aren't colored with any preconceived notions. This can be extremely valuable to your journey.

2. *Therapists are trained.* One of the best gifts a counselor has is training. It often can be confusing trying to parse out your own behavior and thoughts and what they all mean. But a good therapist is educated to see and assess you from a place of wisdom, which ultimately will keep you from wasting time going down unhealthy paths and instead direct you toward a healthier life.

3. *Therapy is a safe place.* The world can feel dangerous, especially when it comes to opening up and working through your issues. You will want to work through them with people who love you, but wise and trustworthy people are few and far between. In an age when you can get "canceled" for saying the wrong thing, therapy gives

you a place to process the real, raw, and sometimes messy thoughts you have about life. It offers a safe place to be human, away from judgment and condemnation. This will ultimately help you think and act more productively because you have a healthy outlet for your frustrations, questions, and thoughts and no longer bottle things up inside.

A King in Waiting

Before David—the beloved giant-slaying, song-writing, war-winning man after God's own heart—became king, he spent years waiting. Samuel anointed David to become king when he was only fifteen, but it wasn't for more than a decade after God made his choice that David found himself where he was always meant to be. For years David spent his time not as a king surrounded by other kings and queens but as a humble shepherd boy surrounded by dumb sheep.

I sometimes wonder if David felt like I often have, asking himself, "Will my great 'destiny' ever take place? Or am I simply going to be here in these quiet fields forever?"

But in reading David's story in Scripture, I noticed that while David waited for his time, he didn't waste his time. In the years between the prophecy placed over David and his actually becoming king, David chose over and over again to respond to God even in the boring and monotonous moments and to use his time in practice for the calling God had on David's life.

I know all too well the feeling that life will never begin. I can read books, listen to pastors, and memorize verses that assure me of the calling God has on my life, but sometimes it feels like it's taking *so* long. But in reading about King David before he became king, I see a model of how all of us ought to wait.

Waiting well is something we must master. So often when we think of waiting, we think of static, still, boring; in reality, waiting is an opportunity to prepare for the destiny we're called to live out. If we don't use our waiting time well, we might find that when we're finally given the opportunity we've been waiting for, we won't be prepared or ready to take on the responsibilities that come with it. Before David defeated Goliath on a battlefield, he defeated a lion in a field. Before David was a public celebrity with adoring fans, he was a hidden man who worshiped God in private.

God has a story and calling for each one of us kings, but his timing is not our timing. Often when it feels like he's forgotten us, instead, he's offering us an opportunity to prepare—to wait well.

Even Jesus Christ himself waited until he was thirty years old to be about his "Father's business" (Luke 2:49 NKJV). In fact, we don't hear anything about his life between his childhood and the last few years of his life aside from one short description: "Jesus grew in wisdom and in stature and in favor with God and all the people" (Luke 2:52), meaning even Jesus, the hero King of the entire world, had to wait. But we see he waited well. He grew in wisdom, he grew physically, and he cultivated relationships with both people around him and God himself.

As we wait on our thrones, let us look to David and Jesus and learn how to wait well so that when the time comes, we will be ready to step fully into our calling as kings.

KING'S QUESTIONS

1. Do you ever feel like it's taking a long time for your life to start?
2. Do you trust God has a story for you to tell? If so, what could it be?
3. What are some ways you can wait well so you'll be prepared for the journey ahead of you?

Scripture Reading

I waited patiently for the LORD to help me,
  and he turned to me and heard my cry.
He lifted me out of the pit of despair,
  out of the mud and the mire.
He set my feet on solid ground
  and steadied me as I walked along.
He has given me a new song to sing,
  a hymn of praise to our God.
Many will see what he has done and be amazed.
  They will put their trust in the LORD.

Oh, the joys of those who trust the LORD,
  who have no confidence in the proud
  or in those who worship idols.
O LORD my God, you have performed many wonders
    for us.
  Your plans for us are too numerous to list.
  You have no equal.
If I tried to recite all your wonderful deeds,
  I would never come to the end of them.

You take no delight in sacrifices or offerings.
  Now that you have made me listen, I finally
    understand—
  you don't require burnt offerings or sin offerings.
Then I said, "Look, I have come.
  As is written about me in the Scriptures:
I take joy in doing your will, my God,
  for your instructions are written on my heart."

Psalm 40:1–8

KING TIP #27

Goal Chart

Write in the goals you'd like to accomplish over the next five years.

Spiritual Goals:

Reading/Educational Goals:

Fitness Goals:

Relational Goals (Romantic and Friendship):

Travel Goals:

Professional Goals:

Personal Project Goals:

Other:

28 Queens

When it comes to ruling over the kingdom we've been given, one of the most important things we can decide is who we will rule it with. After creating Adam, the first man, and giving him dominion over the earth, God said, "It is not good for the man to be alone. I will make him a helper who is just right for him" (Gen. 2:18). Enter Eve, whom God created as a beautiful and competent partner to rule, alongside Adam, the world he had entrusted to them.

A lot has changed in the thousands of years between now and when those words were written down or spoken. But much remains the same. We men, while competent, are not complete. We need other people, and ideally a companion with whom we can enter into a lifelong commitment to rule and reign over the lives God has given us. But as we've seen over and over again, the people we bind ourselves to, especially in marriage, can have heavy consequences on individual kingdoms, lives, and history. This makes choosing the right partner all the more important. And in a world where there seem to be so few who have caught this vision for the life God has given us, it can feel impossible to find a suitable queen to unite with.

It seems this was a problem even in the days of David, which is why Bathsheba, his wife, shared a list of what to look for in a suitable mate, comparing the blessing of a good woman to that of jewels. She also warns of a harmful one who she states has the power to "ruin kings." This is important!

In Proverbs 31, the future king's mother (listen to your moms!) includes the aspects a woman will display if she is a woman of wisdom and strength, the kind that should be sought out.

Proverbs 31 speaks of a woman who is trustworthy and industrious, who is virtuous and has a strong sense of character, who brings life to the people around her, and whose kindness is evident. One who observes the world with intellectual curiosity so that she may speak wisdom. One who has vision for life and uses the gifts she has for good, who is a willing partner with her king and has the potential to be a loving mother to her children. One who laughs at the future because her faith is in God and who clothes herself in the strength and dignity fit for a queen.

This is the kind of woman Scripture tells us to seek out, commit to, and protect. Of course, no woman is perfect. But look for a woman whose heart is bent toward God's and who will ultimately be someone with whom you can look to God as you journey through life.

From the myriad love stories we've seen for centuries, we can easily believe that love is simply a feeling that will ignite based on nothing more than two charming and beautiful people being attracted to each other. But as the proverb states, "Charm is deceptive, and beauty does not last" (v. 30), and we see evidence of that in the overwhelming number of broken relationships in our modern world. So as we go about choosing a queen, we must go further than skin deep and instead look into women's very hearts and souls.

KING'S QUESTIONS

1. Do you want a partner to do life with? Why or why not?
2. What do you look for when choosing a partner?
3. What things should you add to your list that go beyond simple attraction?

Scripture Reading

Who can find a virtuous and capable wife?
    She is more precious than rubies.
Her husband can trust her,
    and she will greatly enrich his life.
She brings him good, not harm,
    all the days of her life.

She finds wool and flax
    and busily spins it.
She is like a merchant's ship,
    bringing her food from afar.
She gets up before dawn to prepare breakfast for her
      household
    and plan the day's work for her servant girls.

She goes to inspect a field and buys it;
    with her earnings she plants a vineyard.
She is energetic and strong,
    a hard worker.
She makes sure her dealings are profitable;
    her lamp burns late into the night.

Her hands are busy spinning thread,
    her fingers twisting fiber.
She extends a helping hand to the poor
    and opens her arms to the needy.
She has no fear of winter for her household,
    for everyone has warm clothes.

She makes her own bedspreads.
    She dresses in fine linen and purple gowns.
Her husband is well known at the city gates,
    where he sits with the other civic leaders.
She makes belted linen garments
    and sashes to sell to the merchants.

She is clothed with strength and dignity,
    and she laughs without fear of the future.
When she speaks, her words are wise,
    and she gives instructions with kindness.
She carefully watches everything in her household
    and suffers nothing from laziness.

Her children stand and bless her.
    Her husband praises her:
"There are many virtuous and capable women in the world,
    but you surpass them all!"

Charm is deceptive, and beauty does not last;
    but a woman who fears the LORD will be greatly
        praised.
Reward her for all she has done.
    Let her deeds publicly declare her praise.

Proverbs 31:10–31

KING TIP #28

Questions to Ask Yourself before Falling in Love

1. Does she love God?
2. Does she have a relationship with God?
3. Does she display healthy behavior (introspection, self-control, temperance, etc.)?
4. Does she honor my boundaries?
5. Does she encourage me to be my best self?
6. Does she challenge me?
7. Does she value intelligence?
8. Does she have her own unique interests and passions?
9. Does she have interests and passions that are shared with mine?
10. Does she read?
11. Does she value health and fitness?
12. Is she kind to others?
13. Am I attracted to her physically?
14. Am I attracted to her mentally and emotionally?
15. Is she willing to acknowledge her faults and work on them?
16. Does she spend her time with wise people?
17. Is she willing to listen?
18. Is she willing to speak up?
19. Is she wise with money?
20. Does she have a good work ethic?

29 The Wise King

King Solomon was known not only as a wealthy king but also a wise king. As the story goes, God came to Solomon one night and offered him anything his heart desired, and instead of asking for love, riches, fame, or power, Solomon asked for wisdom. God honored and celebrated Solomon's decision by giving him both wisdom and everything else a king could want. God knew Solomon's heart was in the right place, and he would now have the wisdom to know how to utilize his wisdom well.

And he did. He went on to write the lion's share of the book of Proverbs, which still today, across a multitude of cultures and traditions, is considered to be one of the wisest books ever written.

Today, wisdom isn't something you see many chasing after. In most of the messages emerging from culture that tell us what we ought to pursue and acquire, wisdom, intelligence, truth, and intellect aren't included. Instead, the world tells us we should spend our lives chasing after happiness, wealth, respect, popularity, comfort, power, and material prizes. But when we look at the kingdom of God, we see a very different set of priorities.

As a kid I often wondered why Solomon asked for wisdom, and I wondered why God seemed so pleased by his request. I mean, being smart is great and stuff, but aren't there better things to ask for?

But now, as an adult who has been charged with many areas to rule over well and a host of responsibilities, I crave wisdom. I know every choice I make bears consequences, and the more wisdom I have as I make decisions, the better the outcome.

Often we think of wisdom as just being "smart," knowing things, and memorizing facts. But wisdom isn't just about knowing things; it's knowing how to think about the things we know. It goes from a static list of facts to a perspective on life that has a real-world effect.

If we wish to be good rulers of the kingdoms God's given us to reign over, we must be wise. We, like Solomon, must ask for and make it our priority to find wisdom as opposed to all the things the world tells us we should ask for. This might look like creating a reading list we stick to or listening to a recommended podcast or sermon series or joining a book club or Bible study that will consistently sharpen our mind.

However we find it, wisdom is a valuable resource that affects the trajectory of our lives and the choices that make them what they are. Be like Solomon, and learn to desire wisdom above all. When we do, God is pleased and we will better rule the dominion God has given us.

KING'S QUESTIONS

1. Do you think wisdom is really that important to acquire?
2. What does the world think of wisdom? Does it value it or not?
3. What are some ways you can start acquiring and using wisdom in your own life?

Scripture Reading

Blessed are those who find wisdom,
    those who gain understanding,
for she is more profitable than silver
    and yields better returns than gold.
She is more precious than rubies;
    nothing you desire can compare with her.
Long life is in her right hand;
    in her left hand are riches and honor.
Her ways are pleasant ways,
    and all her paths are peace.
She is a tree of life to those who take hold of her;
    those who hold her fast will be blessed.

By wisdom the Lord laid the earth's foundations,
    by understanding he set the heavens in place;
by his knowledge the watery depths were divided,
    and the clouds let drop the dew.

My son, do not let wisdom and understanding out of your
        sight,
    preserve sound judgment and discretion;
they will be life for you,
    an ornament to grace your neck.
Then you will go on your way in safety,
    and your foot will not stumble.
When you lie down, you will not be afraid;
    when you lie down, your sleep will be sweet.
Have no fear of sudden disaster
    or of the ruin that overtakes the wicked,
for the Lord will be at your side
    and will keep your foot from being snared.

Proverbs 3:13–26 NIV

KING TIP #29

Theological Book List

Theology means the study of God. In my humble opinion, few things are as important as studying who God is, who God is not, and who God is to us. Studying God is one of the most important aspects to becoming wise. So here are some books that can help you begin the journey of discovering who God is.

1. *The Holy Bible*
2. *Mere Christianity* by C. S. Lewis
3. *Bright Evening Star* by Madeleine L'Engle
4. *Confessions* by Augustine
5. *The Religious Sense* by Father Luigi Giussani
6. *Orthodoxy* by G. K. Chesterton
7. *The Cost of Discipleship* by Dietrich Bonhoeffer
8. *Knowing God* by J. I. Packer
9. *How Should We Then Live?* by Francis Schaeffer
10. *The Jesus Way* by Eugene Peterson

New Name

A name is a powerful thing. It's not just a title or something to categorize us. A name holds identity. We cringe at some names when we hear them spoken because of who we identify with them, while other names bring us joy, excitement, and peace because of who they are attached to. In times past, and in many cultures still today, it was a very real thing to judge someone by their name. So when someone "brought shame" on a name, it affected everyone who bore it.

Names are powerful, and most often we don't choose them ourselves: they are chosen for us. I used to hate my name. I didn't know many boys with the same name as me, and I wanted to be called Jack because, for whatever reason, in my mind that name represented the kind of man I wanted to be. As I grew up, I learned to like the uniqueness of my name, but I also began to realize that whatever I did would be associated with my name forever. That was exciting when I thought about all the great things I wanted to do but distressing when I focused on all the destructive things I was capable of. So in thinking about how my life and choices would affect the name I bore, I found fear and sometimes regret in the immovability of it. Fear because I know I am imperfect and prone to mistakes. And regret from the times my worries were proven valid.

At times, I wish I had a different name. Sometimes I feel the choices I've made and the things I've done have tarnished the name I hold, and the only way to be free, start over, and become new would be to have an entire identity change, a new name. But changing our name means very little, since names that mean something are given to us, not made up out of our own volition. It seems God knows this too.

Throughout Scripture, I am struck by the regularity with which God changed people's names. It started in the oldest Scriptures when he changed Abram to Abraham, then continued all the way to Jesus's time when he renamed Simon, Peter, then Saul, Paul. And with the new name, God also provided a new life, a new start, and a new identity.

Perhaps like me, you long to not be under the curse of what your name has become associated with. Perhaps like me, you no longer want to carry the weight of the mistakes made under the banner of the name you hold. If you feel this way, there is good news! God promises that in following him, we can have a new life, a new beginning, a new chance to get up and no longer be defined by all the mistakes of yesterday. Lamentations 3:22–23 says,

> The faithful love of the LORD never ends!
> His mercies never cease.
> Great is his faithfulness;
> his mercies begin afresh each morning.

Metaphorically speaking (perhaps even literally), God offers us a new name—a clean one that no longer has to be tied to our mistakes but is instead tied to what he says about us, including that we are loved, redeemed, and valued. The letters in our name might not have changed, but the meaning has. We need only accept.

If you are longing for a new beginning, a new defining factor of who you are, take God up on his offer for a new name—one that will define you with his goodness, love, care, power, and strength.

KING'S QUESTIONS

1. Have you ever wanted to start over? To be someone different? If so, when?
2. Have you ever wanted to change your name? Why?
3. What would it feel like to go through life with a new title not tied to your mistakes?

Scripture Reading

Praise the LORD!

How good to sing praises to our God!
　　How delightful and how fitting!
The LORD is rebuilding Jerusalem
　　and bringing the exiles back to Israel.
He heals the brokenhearted
　　and bandages their wounds.
He counts the stars
　　and calls them all by name.
How great is our Lord! His power is absolute!
　　His understanding is beyond comprehension!
The LORD supports the humble,
　　but he brings the wicked down into the dust.

Psalm 147:1–6

KING TIP #30
Royal Name Generator

"_____ (your first name) the _____"

Birth month:

    January—King

    February—Prince

    March—Duke

    April—Knight

    May—Baron

    June—Sir

    July—Lord

    August—Emperor

    September—Count

    October—Marquis

    November—Councilor

    December—Viscount

First letter of your first name:

    A Great

    B Kind

    C Protector

    D Valiant

    E Wise

    F Tender

    G Fierce

    H Peaceful

    I Intelligent

    J Funny

K Terrible

L Curious

M Avenger

N Noble

O Innocent

P Skillful

Q Silent

R Bold

S Tender

T Romantic

U Loving

V Adventurer

W Explorer

X Thoughtful

Y Artistic

Z Lively

Put On the Armor

Kings throughout history knew that keeping the beauty, freedom, goodness, and joy alive in their kingdom took a fight. The peace inside the borders of their kingdom could and would be attacked at a moment's notice. Because of this knowledge, every good king and knight knew to keep their armor near.

Today, in our personal lives, it can feel like a far cry from the times of swords and sweeping battles. But we are in a conflict, nonetheless—every day and in many ways. The darkness of the world—depression, laziness, destructive habits, despair, addiction, capitulation, peer pressure, and more—threatens the goodness of our domains. These enemies seek to destroy the light in our lives, making it so we must wear our armor daily.

In Scripture, we find the apostle Paul reflects this in his words: "For we are not fighting against flesh-and-blood enemies, but against evil rulers and authorities of the unseen world, against mighty powers in this dark world, and against evil spirits in the heavenly places" (Eph. 6:12). He shows that our war isn't against physical foes who seek to harm our bodies but rather the spirits that seek to destroy our hearts.

He goes on to tell us that because of the kind of enemies we are fighting, we ought to put on a particular kind of armor:

Therefore, put on every piece of God's armor so you will be able to resist the enemy in the time of evil. Then after the battle you will still be standing firm. Stand your ground, putting on the belt of truth and the body armor of God's righteousness. For shoes, put on the peace that comes from the Good News so that you will be fully prepared. In addition to all of these, hold up the shield of faith to stop the fiery arrows of the devil. Put on salvation as your helmet, and take the sword of the Spirit, which is the word of God. (vv. 13–17)

As kings, we must be ready to defend ourselves and fight against the darkness of the world, the kind that threatens the light and goodness in our minds, hearts, families, and lives. We do this by putting on the armor of God so we will be ready and equipped to overcome whatever foe this world might send our way.

KING'S QUESTIONS

1. Are you equipped to fight the battles in your own life?
2. Are you wearing armor that will protect you and enable you to overcome?
3. How can you become more equipped in the knowledge of how to put on the armor of God?

Scripture Reading

O Lord, oppose those who oppose me.
    Fight those who fight against me.
Put on your armor, and take up your shield.
    Prepare for battle, and come to my aid.

Lift up your spear and javelin
>against those who pursue me.
Let me hear you say,
>"I will give you victory!"
Bring shame and disgrace on those trying to kill me;
>turn them back and humiliate those who want to harm
>me.
Blow them away like chaff in the wind—
>a wind sent by the angel of the Lord.
Make their path dark and slippery,
>with the angel of the Lord pursuing them.
I did them no wrong, but they laid a trap for me.
>I did them no wrong, but they dug a pit to catch me.
So let sudden ruin come upon them!
>Let them be caught in the trap they set for me!
>Let them be destroyed in the pit they dug for me.

Then I will rejoice in the Lord.
>I will be glad because he rescues me.
With every bone in my body I will praise him:
>"Lord, who can compare with you?
Who else rescues the helpless from the strong?
>Who else protects the helpless and poor from those
>who rob them?"

Psalm 35:1–10

KING TIP #31

The Armor of God

A final word: Be strong in the Lord and in his mighty power. Put on all of God's armor so that you will be able to stand firm against all strategies of the devil. For we are not fighting against flesh-and-blood enemies, but against evil rulers and authorities of the unseen world, against mighty powers in this dark world, and against evil spirits in the heavenly places.

Therefore, put on every piece of God's armor so you will be able to resist the enemy in the time of evil. Then after the battle you will still be standing firm. Stand your ground, putting on the belt of truth and the body armor of God's righteousness. For shoes, put on the peace that comes from the Good News so that you will be fully prepared. In addition to all of these, hold up the shield of faith to stop the fiery arrows of the devil. Put on salvation as your helmet, and take the sword of the Spirit, which is the word of God.

Ephesians 6:13–17

1. *Belt of truth.* We put on God's truth so our whole armor will be intact rather than falling apart by believing the lies this world gives us.

2. *Body armor of God's righteousness.* For our body armor, which guards our vital organs, we choose God's righteousness to guide our choices and protect our hearts.

3. *Shoes of peace.* We let peace guide our steps as we seek to avoid the violence and chaos of the world. God's peace will give us a steady and sure step.

4. *Shield of faith.* Our continual faith in God will protect us from the arrows the evil of the world will hurl at us. We know he will defend us from the crumbling chaos and wrath of the world.

5. *Helmet of salvation.* We can let our minds rest, knowing that our salvation is secured by God's grace no matter what.

6. *Sword of the Spirit.* We wield not a physical sword but a spiritual one. Scripture makes clear that the sword of the Spirit is the Word of God—the one offensive weapon we employ.

# Cracks in the Armor

As kings in the world today, we are in constant battle. We are fighting for provision, goodness, our families, our jobs, our faith, and our morality. Like the kings and warriors of the past, as we become better men, we learn how to fight these battles and stand up to the darkness of the world. But there comes a time when we are worn out, wounded, and in need of care, when we return home, having either won or lost, and we must take off our armor. But this is more easily said than done.

After spending our lives on the defensive, always ready for the next attack, we often find that putting down our shields to pay attention to our wounds is harder than we thought. Today, men face countless struggles in so many areas—and each of these battles takes a toll, wearing us out and wounding us. But so many of us don't know how to press pause. In practicing only fighting, we have often forgotten how to heal.

Vulnerability is classically hard for men, and even harder for ones who've spent their lives fighting. We have become so accustomed to protecting and guarding ourselves, we often don't know how to receive help and healing from ourselves, from the ones around us, or from God.

But when we are wounded and don't pay attention to the injury, it will only worsen and make us weaker until we are able to address it. Our ability to win the conflicts that rage on will be directly tied to our ability to heal from harm.

Taking off our armor, be it metal or mental, can be scary. It makes us vulnerable and uncomfortable. For some of us, being vulnerable is less comfortable than fighting. But for God to do his healing work in us so we can actually overcome the darkness in our world, we must practice taking off our armor. For knights and kings, this took place in the king's chambers or sickroom. For us today, perhaps it can happen in therapy or counseling, by opening up to a good friend, or through prayer.

The war is raging, and we must confront the foes on our kingdom's doorsteps. But to do this well, we must pay attention to our wounds before we pick up our swords. We must repair our armor before we can use it, and to repair our armor we must be brave enough to take it off. In so many stories, it's the cracks in the armor that have gone unfixed, our Achilles' heels that cause the hero to lose the fight.

To become strong, we must learn to be vulnerable. We must take off our armor and heal before we put it on again to fight.

KING'S QUESTIONS

1. Do you struggle with being vulnerable? Why or why not?
2. Do you find it easier to fight than to seek help?
3. Where are some places you can take off your armor to heal?

Scripture Reading

Oh, the joys of those who are kind to the poor!
    The LORD rescues them when they are in trouble.
The LORD protects them
    and keeps them alive.
He gives them prosperity in the land
    and rescues them from their enemies.

The LORD nurses them when they are sick
    and restores them to health.

Psalm 41:1–3

KING TIP #32

The Best Places to Escape and Recoup

The world can be a hard and tiring place. You must find places where you can heal, talk to God, and recoup, or else the stress will take you down.

Below are some of the very best places to find that peace.

1. *In nature.* Being outside in God's creation, away from all man's noise and chaos, is one of the best places to recoup. In the silence and beauty of God's handiwork, often it is more possible to unwind and reflect than when you are stuck in the hustle and bustle of everyday life. Maybe this means taking a hike in the forest to see some views that will bring your mind rest. Perhaps you need to rent a cabin for a weekend so you can pray and reflect. Or possibly you should just go for a walk in a nearby park. When you let

yourself exist in nature, very often you will hear God's voice and feel his healing more easily.

2. *At home.* Home is supposed to be a safe place in a stormy world. A place where you can find refuge. Many who spend countless hours working, attending school, or going to social events have either forgotten or neglected the power of existing in a warm, comforting place. Home can be a place where, if you put some effort and time into making it so, you can disconnect from the hustle and bustle of modern life and find peace, retreat, and comfort. Perhaps it's time for you to make the place you live a space that will offer you a chance to rest (see King Tip #17).

3. *While traveling.* Sometimes getting away really is just what the doctor ordered. While it can take a bit more effort and resources than the previous options, traveling to a new area can help you detach from the stresses in your life and connect with yourself and God. Traveling opens your eyes to new ways of thinking and living and breaks the monotonous routines that are often a source of pain. When you venture out the door, you give your mind, heart, and soul a chance to find fresh inspiration and new ways of thinking and healing.

 # The Value of Silence

Royal rulers are known for many things—their might, presence, and influence. But one thing that rarely makes the list is their silence. In ages past, a king would often make decrees to his people with grand displays and roaring horns. When confronted, kings could be counted on to speak up and make their opinions known, lest anyone think them weak. They were the center of attention in meetings, and whatever the king said held the most weight and had to be listened to.

But then Jesus, the King of Kings, showed us a very different way. Of course, he spoke when he needed to, sharing truth and wisdom, but then we see Jesus often used very few words when confronted by his enemies and scarcely said a thing as he healed people. Sometimes he disappeared altogether, saying nothing to his disciples. When he spoke, his words meant something—perhaps because he knew when to be silent.

We live now in an age in which everyone is talking all the time. We watch talk shows and political debates, we listen to personalities talk nonstop on podcasts. And it's no longer just the media that get to spew their opinions regularly; it's all of us. On our social media posts, through comments and messages, on the phone, through text, and even via in-person arguments. But if we step back and look, we see only an endless chaos of words: everyone is talking and no one is listening to each other.

To be good and wise kings, we must utilize the art of silence like Jesus did. Proverbs 17:28 says, "Even fools are thought wise when they keep silent," and it seems we now live in a time when everyone would rather be seen as a fool than learn to hold their tongues and listen.

James 1:19 says, "Understand this, my dear brothers and sisters: You must all be quick to listen, slow to speak, and slow to get angry." We must learn how to be slow to speak, we must learn when to speak, and we must learn when not to speak so that we may both hear and understand what is going on around us and learn the weight our words have on the world. It is only when we close our mouths and listen that we can hear from God and other sources. Then when we speak, we will actually have something to say.

Let us be kings who know how to best utilize silence so when we do speak, our words will be ones of weight and wisdom.

KING'S QUESTIONS

1. Do you think there is value in silence and knowing when to hold our tongues?
2. Are you good at sitting in silence and listening? Or do you have trouble?
3. What are reasons to learn the value of silence?

Scripture Reading

Hiding hatred makes you a liar;
  slandering others makes you a fool.

Too much talk leads to sin.
  Be sensible and keep your mouth shut.

The words of the godly are like sterling silver;
  the heart of a fool is worthless.

The words of the godly encourage many,
  but fools are destroyed by their lack of common sense.

The blessing of the Lord makes a person rich,
  and he adds no sorrow with it.

Proverbs 10:18–22

KING TIP #33

How to Meditate

Meditation is something the modern church hasn't taught or understood well. Many of us think it's done only in far-off countries and yoga studios. But meditation is talked about and encouraged throughout Scripture (for example, see Psalm 1:2). Meditation can have powerful benefits in your life, in bringing both peace and a closer connection with God. Below you'll find steps for using meditation in your own journey.

1. *Set a time limit.* You don't have to dedicate hours to meditating. Maybe just five or fifteen minutes is enough. But when you set a time limit, you give yourself a

goal to reach, and that will keep you accountable and involved.

2. *Get in position.* You want to be comfortable, but not so much that you fall asleep. You want to find a position that will allow your mind to stay active while your body is at peace. One of the best positions is sitting cross-legged, your hands at rest on your knees and your back straight.

3. *Pick your view.* When meditating, you will want to find a non-distracting view to rest your eyes on—maybe a peaceful picture or a beautiful landscape or even a blank wall. You can also close your eyes. This will eliminate the distractions around you so you can better focus on the task at hand.

4. *Put on some music or noise.* This part is optional, but putting on a peaceful sound like a recording of the ocean waves, the wind, a creek flowing, or a gentle instrumental song that brings you peace can help you be in the moment.

5. *Breathe.* Calm your breath by breathing deeply in and out. This will relax your entire body, including your heart and mind.

6. *Clear your mind.* The stress and hustle of life give you many things to worry about. But as you meditate, let your mind be in a place where your fears and the noise of the world take a back seat for just a while so you can rest, connect with God, and clear out the toxicity.

7. *Repeat a phrase.* A beneficial thing you can do as you learn to meditate is have a phrase you repeat to yourself over and over. This will combat all the other accusatory, anxious, stressful voices in your head and replace them with a comforting and true set of words. Saying a truth about God or yourself is a good place to start. Try something like, "I am loved by God" or "God is always with me." This practice can be very impactful.

 # Living Free

So much of royal life seems like it must be confined within pre-determined expectations of behavior and lists of to-dos and not-to-dos. To some, becoming a king might seem like it takes away one's personal autonomy and replaces it with a rigid monotony of responsibility and structured compliance in a boring paint-by-number life.

We live in a world where so many aspects of our lives have been labeled and structured. Society seems to want to control our every move and beat us into submission to live a predictable and uninspired life. I have so many friends who feel trapped in their schooling, jobs, or other situations. Each longs for more than a cookie-cutter life. With all the expectations and responsibility that come with taking on the title of king, we may fear that same controlling and lifeless duty might exist.

But in reality, while claiming our crown does come with responsibility, it also comes with a chance to live truly free. When we respond to God's call in our lives, we step into the ability to live freely. We are not only able but also encouraged by God to pursue our passions, search our deepest desires, and live out an adventure. As kings, we have been asked by God not to live by the world's boring and suffocating boundaries. God is a creative and wild God, and he created us in his own image to follow in his footsteps.

When we respond to God's offer of a meaningful life and choose to act with adventurous purpose, it will take us away from the constraining messages of the world and give us a chance to live our lives as who we were made to be. To find the wild and passionate parts of ourselves and to live those out in a way that honors God and brings goodness to the world.

David was criticized when he broke the rules of society and danced in the streets praising God. People looked at him like he was crazy and mocked him. But God honored David because David was living out with passion who God made him to be (see 2 Sam. 6:14–22).

When I decided what to do with my future as a young king, I chose the opposite direction of the world's expectation. Instead, I took the road less traveled and discovered why I was created and decided to live that "why" out in my domain, despite many doubting I would be able to succeed.

God created the wild wind, roaring seas, and epic mountains. And that same God made you! It's humans who made colorless walls and dead-end jobs. But with God we can begin to live a full, beautiful life of adventure and purpose when we start looking at our work (no matter what our job is) in a way that can be deeply meaningful right where we are.

It is often scary to live free and break out of the safe constraints the world offers, but it is always better. For some of us, this might look like choosing a new college major that inspires our hearts instead of the one we have been told we should pursue. For others, this looks like finding a job that allows us to live into the passions of our hearts instead of the safe one that offers more money but no purpose. And for some of us, this looks like hiking in the mountains to see the limitless and wild beauty God has created.

But whatever choosing to live beyond the constraints of this world looks like for you, it will bring the freedom to live out who you were actually made to be—and that will be the adventure of a lifetime.

KING'S QUESTIONS

1. Do you feel constrained in life right now? If so, how or why?

2. Do you think that living freely is something worth pursuing?

3. How will you take steps to live out who you were made to be instead of who you are expected to be?

Scripture Reading

Shout with joy to the LORD, all the earth!
    Worship the LORD with gladness.
    Come before him, singing with joy.
Acknowledge that the LORD is God!
    He made us, and we are his.
    We are his people, the sheep of his pasture.
Enter his gates with thanksgiving;
    go into his courts with praise.
    Give thanks to him and praise his name.
For the LORD is good.
    His unfailing love continues forever,
    and his faithfulness continues to each generation.

Psalm 100

KING TIP #34

How to Escape Being Tied Up

We've all seen it in movies—the good guy gets captured and tied up but, through some quick thinking and skill, escapes and defeats the bad guy. But how possible is it to actually escape like a magician out of ropes or zip ties? Below is the best way to get out of a sticky situation if you should ever find yourself tied up!

1. Present your hands/wrists to your captor with your hands/ fists facing down while clenching your fists. This will widen the area they are tying.

2. After being secured, turn your hands to face each other and unclench your fists. This will provide you enough slack that you should be able to finagle your hands free, and if other areas have been tied up you can now free them.

3. Some bonds can be broken with enough force by raising your hands and slamming them down on your legs while pulling your wrists and arms in opposite directions.

4. If you still find yourself bound, even after implementing the first options, you can try to find a rough surface, like a sharp table edge or broken glass. Carefully rub the ties over the sharp object over a long period of time to break your binds. It will take patience and repetition, but this method can prove effective in a tight spot.

EXTRA TIP: If you find your hands bound behind your back, instead of trying to implement any of the above methods, you can bring your hands below your rear and under your legs so you will have your hands in front of you for an easier escape.

Smashing Idols

Throughout the book of Exodus in the Old Testament, we see a nomadic people following their leaders through foreign lands and unknown places. They were God's chosen people looking for the kingdom promised them. In many of the places they wandered, they found these foreign nations didn't worship the one true God; they bowed down to idols. (An idol is something other than God that people give their affection, time, and hope to in an effort to get the things they want.) But unlike the living God, idols had no power, and ultimately the worship of them led these nations to ruin.

God told his people over and over never to be swayed by the pagan cultures worshiping idols. It may have looked fun, and the idol worshipers were able to live how they wanted in all the sinful ways they pleased, but God knew how destructive this path was and warned his people to stay far away. But time and again, because of their weak faith, God's chosen people traded their one true God, who gave them guidance and wisdom, for the easy and alluring statues that gave them permission to do what they pleased and promised them things they never should have had.

Every time God's people turned away from him and allowed these foreign idols to take his place, destruction followed. But every time they turned their hearts to him and trusted him, even when it was hard, they found blessing.

We, too, live in a world of idols. They don't look like the golden calves or stone statues from past millennia, but our world has created its own idols. We've chosen to put our hope in things other than God. Things like sex, fame, money, politics, success, and power. Daily we see people worshiping these things instead of the God who created them. And just as often we see how disastrous the worship of these things is. In the headlines and our social media feeds, we see the reality of brokenness, abuse, envy, corruption, selfishness, and more.

Idols look good to many of us. They promise us what we want but don't tell of the consequences. Whereas God can sometimes feel far away or invisible, he promises only the best for us. But he does require that we have faith and do things that can be hard. It's easy but destructive to worship idols; it's far more difficult but better to choose to worship God and allow him to be our sole source of guidance. Then we'll find the wisdom and blessing to live as who we were made to be.

KING'S QUESTIONS

1. Do you think humans still struggle with idol worship? If so, what are some examples?

2. What are some modern idols that tempt you away from God?

3. What are some ways you can remove the idols from your life?

Scripture Reading

Your name, LORD, endures forever,
  your renown, LORD, through all generations.
For the LORD will vindicate his people
  and have compassion on his servants.

The idols of the nations are silver and gold,
  made by human hands.
They have mouths, but cannot speak,
  eyes, but cannot see.
They have ears, but cannot hear,
  nor is there breath in their mouths.
Those who make them will be like them,
  and so will all who trust in them.

Psalm 135:13–18 NIV

KING TIP #35
Most Common Modern Idols

We often think of idols as little gold statues like we read about in Scripture. But today, we have made all sorts of new idols to be aware of. Below you will find some of the most common modern-day idols you need to watch out for.

1. *Money*. Money is one of the oldest and most powerful idols. The pursuit of it can take your attention and whole life and ultimately draw you away from God if you let it become your life's focus.

2. *Fame/popularity*. Receiving recognition and praise from the world and people around you can be a powerful draw,

especially with the world's focus on celebrity culture and social media fame, but it can corrupt you and your desires if you are not careful.

3. *Power.* Power, especially when you feel powerless, can feel like a solution to your problems and a way to control the world around you. But this is not God's way. The worship of power can take you down paths that will change you and put you in positions where you seek to do God's job.

4. *Comfort.* Comfort, while not inherently wrong, can become an idol when you allow your whole life to be dictated by its allure. Comfort can keep you from doing the things you are called to and lull you into a false sense of safety at the expense of your calling.

5. *Love.* Love is a wonderful thing, but when not connected to God, it can quickly become an idol. You can spend your whole life trying to get people to love you, romantically or otherwise. When you spend all your time and effort trying to acquire it, you will find yourself serving a master that will bring you only to destructive places.

6. *Work.* You were made to work and use your gifts to build the kingdom of God, but when you allow work to become an idol—letting it take up all your time, effort, and energy—you will watch it steal from other areas of your life, like your family, rest time, and your relationship with God.

7. *Physical things.* Nice houses, cars, clothes, shoes, and other objects aren't evil in and of themselves. But if you aren't careful, you can become far too obsessed with their presence or lack thereof in your life. Things aren't bad, but they cannot be what is most important, because ultimately everything physical will pass away; God will not.

Who's to Blame?

Blame has been a part of human history for as long as people have roamed the earth. Both peasant and king have sought to blame their problems, mistakes, and troubles on someone else. Peasants blame their rulers for their hardships, while kings blame their enemies. And today we live in a world that encourages us to take no responsibility for the hardships in our lives but find people, places, or situations to blame instead. And of course we want to do that; it's so much easier to look to someone or something else as the cause of our troubles, because then we can sit back and expect them to fix everything.

Each of our lives is filled with hardships that take different forms, all the result of a broken world. And when we come in contact with God, he has sympathy and love for us and the difficulties we've gone through. But unlike the world, he asks us to do something about them.

The world tries to convince us that we are victims and have no power over our situations. But God, unlike the world, says that with him we actually have agency to change our world, to better our circumstances, and to heal the broken places in our lives. He empowers us to act with him to heal, grow, and redeem the fractured places of our lives.

Taking responsibility for our lives can be hard, and it's natural to want to buy into the world's lie that there's just nothing we can do about our circumstances. But that's not a true message or one of strength or empowerment. As kings, we mustn't give in to the easy way of living as a victim of our circumstances; instead, we must take God's hand and assert agency over the circumstances we have been given.

Because we have a strong God who walks with us, we have the power to overcome anything the world throws at us. Philippians 4:12–13 says, "I know how to live on almost nothing or with everything. I have learned the secret of living in every situation, whether it is with a full stomach or empty, with plenty or little. For I can do everything through Christ, who gives me strength." It will take fighting, it will take work, but the ones who refuse to give in to the mindset of victimhood and take on the empowering strength God has created them with will taste victory in their lives.

No matter what has happened to you, where you've been, or what you've gone through, you don't have to live as a victim. With God's strength, you can begin the process of healing, fighting back, and overcoming this world's darkness. Take heart!

KING'S QUESTIONS

1. Are you ever tempted to give up and believe you are a victim with no power? If so, when?
2. What things in your life do you want to overcome, heal from, and change?
3. How can you begin to practice seeing yourself as someone who's not a victim?

Scripture Reading

Some sat in darkness, in utter darkness,
  prisoners suffering in iron chains,
because they rebelled against God's commands
  and despised the plans of the Most High.
So he subjected them to bitter labor;
  they stumbled, and there was no one to help.
Then they cried to the LORD in their trouble,
  and he saved them from their distress.
He brought them out of darkness, the utter darkness,
  and broke away their chains.
Let them give thanks to the LORD for his unfailing love
  and his wonderful deeds for mankind,
for he breaks down gates of bronze
  and cuts through bars of iron.

Some became fools through their rebellious ways
  and suffered affliction because of their iniquities.

They loathed all food
  and drew near the gates of death.
Then they cried to the LORD in their trouble,
  and he saved them from their distress.
He sent out his word and healed them;
  he rescued them from the grave.
Let them give thanks to the LORD for his unfailing love
  and his wonderful deeds for mankind.
Let them sacrifice thank offerings
  and tell of his works with songs of joy.

Psalm 107:10–22 NIV

KING TIP #36

Four Steps to Not Living as a Victim

There's not a person alive who hasn't or won't experience the pain and brokenness of a fallen world. This reality may make you want to give up and live as a victim. But to really take up the calling and kingship God has called you to, with God's help, you must find a way to move beyond being a victim and toward being a victor. Below you will find the steps to finally break free of the victim mentality and embrace the victor mindset, which will give you agency in the world and the ability to live out a great story.

1. *Accept.* Accept the full reality of what has happened to you. Don't try to downplay or ignore it. Face it and call it out for what it is. In confronting the reality of the situation, you can work through your feelings and begin to understand them.

2. *Process.* Process the situation. Don't try to stuff down your emotions. If you're sad, be sad; if you're angry, be angry. Working through your pain will ultimately free you from it and allow it to stay in the past, not with you in your present or future.

3. *Heal.* Do the work to heal from the pain and hurt you have felt by using therapy, journaling, resting, joining a group, or traveling. Take time to let your mind and heart heal. If you don't, you'll be limping through life with a broken leg. Being victimized can make you feel powerless. But when you accept, process, and heal, you begin to realize and live into the power you have—power to make changes in your life and do good in the world around you.

4. *Act.* After going through the hard journey out of victimhood and into realizing your own strength, it's time to actually live through the power you have and to actively

(even in small ways) shape the world around you. Write that book, help that person, stand up for the weak, protect yourself.

Moving from victim to victor can be a long, hard journey, but one that will ultimately leave you with less pain, more agency, and the ability to shape the world you live in for the better. It's easy to be bitter and angry at the world for the pain it's caused you. But it's beautiful to heal, rise again, and own your life.

Process
and Patience

We live in a world of instant gratification. Venturing across the country used to take months, even years, and was treacherous. Now we can fly safely around the world in a matter of hours, traversing mountains and deserts while reading a magazine. Understanding complex situations, Scripture, and philosophy used to be of high value, and now we allow headlines, Instagram posters, and "isms" to inform us. Our smartphones give us access to anything we might need to know at the touch of a button. Our food used to take days to gather, as fields had to be tended and animals had to be hunted for meat. Then it took hours to make the food. Now when we want to eat, we have instant access to prepackaged snacks, frozen microwave meals, and fast-food drive-through combos. Romance and love, which used to be a long and slow process of pursuit and patience, has turned into incautiously swiping yes for a date we might end up ghosting later.

Technology and progress are wonderful and have made life better in many ways, but they have also come with a price. We now believe if something doesn't happen quickly and easily, it's not worth pursuing. We don't work the muscle of patience and we don't learn the lesson of process. The idea of instant gratification has even found its way into our churches and pulpits, where we're told if we say the right prayer, we will instantly get the money, the relationship, the body we desire. God has ceased to be someone with whom we have a relationship and is instead a vending machine we expect to give us what we want.

But looking back over history at the kings and heroes, inventors and world-changers, I'm struck by how many of them knew the value of process and were patient and dedicated enough to let their work in the world take the time it needed to grow into something beautiful and effective. And as I see how God has worked in the lives of the leading characters in Scripture—both kings and peasants, the ones he used to tell his story—what I see is the presence of process. God can do anything on any timetable he chooses, but I see through his Word that he likes us taking one step at a time to discover his will.

As we step into the destiny God has called us to, we may be tempted to think we should have everything we desire. But as we become the kings we were created to be, we must remember God's love of process. We must allow his work to take place in our hearts, minds, bodies, and lives little by little, step-by-step. We have the option not to follow God because we're impatient or bored, but the ones who faithfully trust his work of process will reap the rewards of his goodness.

Fast food might be quicker, dating apps might be easier, and flying might be faster, but none of these things can rival the beauty and fullness of a gourmet meal, a lifelong romance, or a cross-country road trip. In the same way, it might be less difficult to take the easy and quick way in life, but it will never compare to the pleasure and joy of arriving in the place God has prepared for you to rule.

KING'S QUESTIONS

1. Do you think instant gratification is a good thing? Why or why not?

2. For what things in your life are you having to learn to trust a slower process?

3. In what areas of your life can you start trusting God step-by-step?

Scripture Reading

Do not fret because of those who are evil
  or be envious of those who do wrong;
for like the grass they will soon wither,
  like green plants they will soon die away.

Trust in the LORD and do good;
  dwell in the land and enjoy safe pasture.
Take delight in the LORD,
  and he will give you the desires of your heart.

Commit your way to the LORD;
  trust in him and he will do this:
He will make your righteous reward shine like the dawn,
  your vindication like the noonday sun.

Be still before the LORD
  and wait patiently for him;
do not fret when people succeed in their ways,
  when they carry out their wicked schemes.

Psalm 37:1–7 NIV

KING TIP #37
Bucket List

One of the best ways to wait is to look ahead to what could be. Making a bucket list while you are waiting is a wonderful way to have things to strive and hope for! Below, fill out your own list of things you'd like to experience in the future.

1. A far-off place I would like to go someday:

   _____

2. A hike/place I would like to take/explore:

   _____

3. A place I'd like to live:

   _____

4. A personal project I would like to complete:

   _____

5. An activity (like skydiving) I would like to try once:

   _____

6. A hobby I'd like to take up:

   _____

7. A person I'd like to meet:

   _____

8. A play/show/concert I'd like to see:

   _____

9. An object I'd like to make with my hands:

   _____

10. A food I'd like to try:

   _____

11. A book I'd like to read:

   _____

12. A game I'd like to play:

   _____

13. A person I'd like to apologize to or work things out with:

   _____

14. A person I'd like to ask out:

   _____

15. A costume I'd like to wear:

   _____

16. A party I'd like to attend:

   _____

17. A class I'd like to take:

   _____

18. Miscellaneous:

   _____

19. Miscellaneous:

   _____

Fear Not

Humans are full of fear. From the beginning of recorded history, we see that humans have been scared of predators, other people, starvation, and the dark. Through the centuries, we have sought to defeat our fears with various means. We invented houses, weapons, farming, and electricity. But in every generation, new things to be scared of arise. Even now, with all our advanced technology and modern hubris, we are still a scared species. We're scared of old age, not finding love, not mattering, losing money, being publicly shamed, being alone. Fear is an intrinsic part of being human, and it's one every king has had to confront to help comfort and lead his people. But how?

Christ, the King of Kings, tended to repeat the things he really wanted us to remember. And one of the things he said over and over again was "fear not." God said "fear not" throughout the Old Testament, the words *don't be afraid* were spoken before Christ's appearance in Luke 1:30, and one of the last things Jesus said to his friends was, "Don't let your hearts be troubled" (John 14:1).

I think God repeats this throughout his Word because he knows how prone to fear we can be. He understands how frail and insecure we are. He recognizes that there is a lot to be fearful of, which is why he reminds us to put our faith in him. And when we do, we find that the fear this world creates fades and the hope he brings grows.

Trusting in God doesn't mean bad things won't happen in our lives. Even Jesus and his disciples endured terrible things and were eventually killed. God tells us not to fear because, ultimately, even though there might be troubles in this world, he has overcome the world and promised us an eternity with him where all the awful things of this world will be undone. We see this in John 14:1–3: "Don't let your hearts be troubled. Trust in God, and trust also in me. There is more than enough room in my Father's home. If this were not so, would I have told you that I am going to prepare a place for you? When everything is ready, I will come and get you, so that you will always be with me where I am."

Our King knows his subjects will be scared. But he asks us to trust in his promises. He asks us to believe he is making everything that is wrong, right. And one day this work will be completed.

We will all face fear of one kind or another. But our King has promised us a future with hope. And when we trust him, his hope—not fear—will rule our lives.

KING'S QUESTIONS

1. Are you a fearful person? If yes, why are you that way?
2. What are you scared of?
3. Do you trust God and the promises of hope he has made?

Scripture Reading

The LORD is my light and my salvation—
    so why should I be afraid?
The LORD is my fortress, protecting me from danger,
    so why should I tremble?

When evil people come to devour me,
    when my enemies and foes attack me,
    they will stumble and fall.
Though a mighty army surrounds me,
    my heart will not be afraid.
Even if I am attacked,
    I will remain confident.

The one thing I ask of the LORD—
    the thing I seek most—
is to live in the house of the LORD all the days of my life,
    delighting in the LORD's perfections
    and meditating in his Temple.
For he will conceal me there when troubles come;
    he will hide me in his sanctuary.
    He will place me out of reach on a high rock.
Then I will hold my head high
    above my enemies who surround me.
At his sanctuary I will offer sacrifices with shouts of joy,
    singing and praising the LORD with music.

Psalm 27:1–6

KING TIP #38

Dealing with Anxiety

Anxiety is a terrible affliction that affects everyone at some point. But you follow a God who says to fear not. So below are some ways you can confront painful anxiety with an intention to find peace and live in better health and freedom:

1. *Breathe.* Even though anxiety lives in the mind, it can affect your body (heightened heart rate, poor posture, tight stomach). When you take a moment to settle your body, it

can also help your mind. Breathing deeply and slowly in through the nose and out through the mouth has a calming effect on your whole mind and body.

2. *Close your eyes.* Sometimes the visual chaos from the world around you can heighten your anxiety, making it harder for you to calm down. When you close your eyes and take deep, focused breaths, you are regaining control of your body and giving your mind a rest so it can better deal with what's happening.

3. *Clasp your hands.* Young children often reach out to a trusted guardian to feel safe. While you won't always be able to reach out and physically touch another person, the simple act of clasping your hands together can calm your mind, especially if you need to squeeze out some of your stress.

4. *Talk to yourself.* Anxiety is often manifested by fearful voices entering your head. It can be helpful to talk truth to the lies that anxiety will tell you. Repeating phrases like "God is in control" or "It's all going to be okay" or "No matter what, I am loved" can combat the voices of fear.

5. *Talk to God.* God promises his people peace in trouble and protection in times of stress. When you pray and ask him to be near, you will find that remembering his presence will help you through your anxiety. Say a small prayer like "God, be with me" to remind yourself he is near.

Follow Your Skills, Not Your Dreams

"Follow your dreams" is a phrase we hear echoed throughout our world today. And as we begin to discover who we were made to be, following our dreams sounds like a good idea. Why wouldn't it be? The phrase is meant to be empowering and inspiring! But I've seen this phrase do more harm than it ever has good.

Very often when I see men living out this quote, I see them come to ruin—not because God doesn't have a destiny for them but because they are following dreams they have no business believing are theirs.

Whether they follow someone else's dream for them or a dream that lives only in fantasy and has no grounding in reality, the end result is often the same. People wind up bitter, frustrated, and having wasted precious time. And they're no further along in discovering who they were meant to be than they were when they began their journey. So should we give up on doing great things, creating a vision for our lives, or believing God has an epic story for us to tell? Absolutely not!

But I put forth that maybe there's a better (albeit longer and not quite as catchy) motto to live by than "Follow your dreams." It's one that will bring purpose, success, and ultimately fulfillment if we see it through. I think instead of learning to follow our dreams, we ought to follow our *skills* and form our dreams around the gifts God has already given us rather than the fantasy of who we wish we were.

God has created all his kings with special talents, personalities, gifts, and skills. Some of us are analytical, others creative. Some of us are good with our hands and others of us excel at business. Some of us are naturally outgoing and personable, and others of us are introverted with a deep interior world. But all of us were made specifically with unique traits God wants to use.

When we follow our skills, our natural gifts, we allow God to shape our dreams out of who we were always supposed to be. But when we operate outside our skills, we create dreams that have nothing to do with the reality of who God created us to be.

We must begin the journey of discovering what we were made to do using our God-given passions, abilities, and skills. From there we can begin to form our dreams using these attributes in a way that brings life to our kingdoms and worlds.

KING'S QUESTIONS

1. Do you believe you were created with particular skills and gifts?
2. What are your skills and gifts?
3. How could you imagine using them for good in the world?

⚜

Scripture Reading

Do you see any truly competent workers?
   They will serve kings
   rather than working for ordinary people.

Proverbs 22:29

KING TIP #39
Finding Your Calling

Finding our calling is something almost all of us desire to do. But in a crazy world with so many options and voices, it can be confusing to pinpoint what exactly we were meant to do. Below are some questions to answer that will give you insight into what it is God might be calling you to do with your life. Ponder how these answers could lead you to discover a path for your life.

1. What do you love doing?

   _____

2. What are you good at?

   _____

3. How do you spend your spare time?

   _____

4. What activities have you found continued success in?

   _____

5. What hobbies are you drawn to?

   _____

6. What have trusted people praised you for?

   _____

7. Are you an introvert or an extrovert?

   _____

8. Do you like working in groups or on your own?

   _____

9. Do you like traveling, staying in one place, or both?

   _____

10. How do you best serve other people?

   _____

11. What breaks your heart?

    _____

12. What issues are you most passionate about seeing addressed in the world?

    _____

40 King of Your Heart

Since the dawn of time, kings have sought to rule other lands. With their armies they would set forth and conquer whatever area was beneficial to their kingdom. The king's decisions and decrees determined whether the kingdom would prosper and bring life or fail and bring destruction and death.

But aside from the physical kingdoms created on earth, another kind of throne is even more important—eternally so. The throne I speak of isn't gilded with any earthly materials like gold or silver, and it doesn't exist inside the halls of a castle. The throne I speak of lives in every person's heart, including yours and mine. And unlike the thrones of the world, we get to decide who sits on this one.

Most people choose to put themselves on the throne of their heart. They decide how best to rule their bodies, minds, and souls. They set up their own little kingdoms run and ruled by themselves. But over and over again, billions upon billions of times, stretching back to the first humans, only destruction follows this kind of kingdom.

There is another who is willing to sit on the throne of our heart—the One who, with wisdom, grace, justice, and love, desires to rule to the benefit of both ourselves and the world we live in. *Our Creator.* God has designed us and given us the option of who sits on the throne of our heart. He offers us the choice of who will rule over our decisions, selections, and domains. And while it feels safe and natural to be the king of our own hearts, many of us know that we ultimately cannot rule ourselves well. Our selfish desires, fearful tendencies, prideful egos, and shortsighted vision will eventually bring us to a place of destruction.

With God's offer comes the promise of redemption for our past mistakes, grace in our imperfect efforts, wisdom in our unknowing, and love in our insecurity. When we allow God to sit on the throne of our heart and through his Word make the decrees that inform our choices, we find that our Creator, knowing always what is ultimately best and most beneficial for us, will rule our heart the way it was meant to be.

God has invited us into his heritage to be king of the domains he has given us, but we will rule well only if we first let him rule our heart. How do we do this? We invite him in and listen to his wisdom in his Word, even when it's hard.

Every heart will have a king sitting on its throne. May we learn to let the God and King of all sit on ours.

KING'S QUESTIONS

1. Who is sitting on the throne of your heart?
2. Do you think you or God will be a better ruler of your soul and life?
3. How can you begin to let God reign over your life?

Scripture Reading

Come, everyone! Clap your hands!
    Shout to God with joyful praise!
For the LORD Most High is awesome.
    He is the great King of all the earth.
He subdues the nations before us,
    putting our enemies beneath our feet.
He chose the Promised Land as our inheritance,
    the proud possession of Jacob's descendants, whom
        he loves.

God has ascended with a mighty shout.
    The LORD has ascended with trumpets blaring.
Sing praises to God, sing praises;
    sing praises to our King, sing praises!
For God is the King over all the earth.
    Praise him with a psalm.
God reigns above the nations,
    sitting on his holy throne.
The rulers of the world have gathered together
    with the people of the God of Abraham.
For all the kings of the earth belong to God.
    He is highly honored everywhere.

Psalm 47

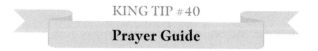

KING TIP #40

Prayer Guide

While your heart might be in the right place, sometimes praying can be difficult to do regularly and thoroughly. Because of the many distractions of life, including wandering thoughts and pressing schedules, you might feel overwhelmed about how to pray. Below you'll find a helpful outline for praying that will keep you focused and guide you to a closer walk with God.

1. *Thanks.* Start your prayer with thanks to God, and go through the things in your life that you are thankful for. Thanking God for your blessings helps you and your mood as you start your conversation with him.

2. *Confession.* It's hard to acknowledge your mistakes and shortcomings, but there is freedom in doing so. When you do confess, your burdens are lifted by knowing you can rely on God's grace and forgiveness.

3. *People.* Praying for people in your life pleases God, as it shows you care for others. This will help you remember that you aren't alone and will take your attention off your own problems for a moment.

4. *Provision.* Asking God for provision and sustenance is essential because it encourages you to bring your needs to him and rely on his help. Ask freely for what you need to do his will. Here you can talk about your dreams and desires and ask him humbly for the means to accomplish what he has asked of you.

5. *Mind/body/soul.* Praying for each of these important parts of yourself allows God into each of them. Praying for wisdom for your mind, health for your body, and comfort for your soul is never a wasted prayer.

AFTERWORD

Continuing the Journey

In every great story is a moment when the hero has to make a choice—a choice to go back to the comfortable and safe place he was or take the road less traveled. The choice to step into the great story of a king can be scary. It will entail pain, struggle, and fighting but ultimately bring about triumph, meaning, and purpose.

Like the heroes of both history and tale, we all have been given a choice. We have been offered the chance to pursue the great stories we were created to live or return to the safe and meaningless lives the world has to offer.

Our Creator God has offered us a part in the grand story he is weaving through history. We have the opportunity to be part of bringing about a new kingdom and ruling it with him: a kingdom of love, grace, beauty, strength, and redemption. But we live right now in a world filled with dominions of darkness, hate, anger, trauma, sadness, and destruction. So, we must follow God on this path that will be hard but great as we overcome the world's darkness with light.

Most want to be part of a great narrative, but not all are willing to do what it takes to live a life of value, a story worth telling. If we want to claim our title as king, if we want to be part of the grand tale, we must choose to take the journey in front of us every day.

May we be kings who follow God in all the big and small areas that compose the story we tell with our lives.

Looking at all it takes to be a king, living into the calling we have in our lives, and making the choices that will allow us to live a bigger and better narrative can be daunting. An almost impossible task. When some look at the way of the King, they like the *idea* of being a king and of reaping the results that come with a life lived with intention and purpose. But when they see the hard work it takes, they decide to choose the easier path, one that doesn't have as many mountains to climb. Yet for those kings willing to take the journey, the view of seeing yourself live into who you were created to be awaits as your reward.

KING'S QUESTIONS

1. Do you believe you were made to tell a great story?
2. What are some things that might keep you from living the narrative God has for you?
3. How will you say yes every day to the journey before you?

Scripture Reading

O Lord, I give my life to you.
  I trust in you, my God!
Do not let me be disgraced,
  or let my enemies rejoice in my defeat.

No one who trusts in you will ever be disgraced,
>   but disgrace comes to those who try to deceive others.

Show me the right path, O LORD;
>   point out the road for me to follow.

Lead me by your truth and teach me,
>   for you are the God who saves me.
>   All day long I put my hope in you.
Remember, O LORD, your compassion and unfailing love,
>   which you have shown from long ages past.
Do not remember the rebellious sins of my youth.
>   Remember me in the light of your unfailing love,
>   for you are merciful, O LORD.

The LORD is good and does what is right;
>   he shows the proper path to those who go astray.
He leads the humble in doing right,
>   teaching them his way.
The LORD leads with unfailing love and faithfulness
>   all who keep his covenant and obey his demands.

Psalm 25:1–10

KING TIP #41

The King's Oath

I vow to live well into my calling of king.
To take seriously the responsibilities God the King of
>   Kings has entrusted to me.
To better myself while serving others daily.
To love the unloved.
To stand up for goodness even when I stand alone.
To fight the battles both in the world and inside my head
>   and heart for the goal of bringing God's goodness and
>   beauty to the world.

To protect the innocent while giving grace to the fallen.

To accept help when I need it and to give it when I am able.

To chase wisdom to deepen my mind and to catch wonder to deepen my soul.

To live confidently in the ways I know to be right while remaining humble enough to always be able to learn.

To act with honor in all my relationships and pursuits.

To use whatever power I might have or obtain for good.

To actively grow in mind, body, and relationship with my Creator.

I vow to follow in God's footsteps to grow into the man and king he has created me to be.

Nathan Clarkson is an award-winning actor, a bestselling author, an indie filmmaker, and a podcast philosopher. He is the author of *Good Man* and coauthor of the *Publishers Weekly* bestselling book *Different*. He lives between the city of New York and the wilds of Colorado.

Ancient Wisdom for the Modern Young Man Stepping into His Story

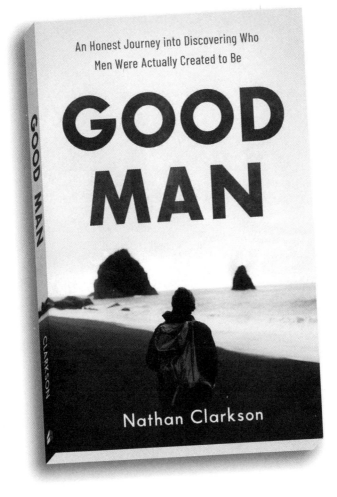

Packed with practical, biblically based advice on real-life issues, *Good Man* helps men base their identity not in who the world says they should be but in who their King says they can be.

Get to know
NATHAN!

Visit **nathanclarkson.me** to learn more.

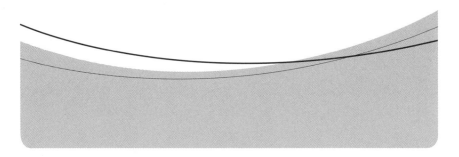